THE PLAINCHANT EVENING PSALTER AND CANTICLES

EDITED BY

FRANCIS BURGESS

MUSICAL DIRECTOR OF THE GREGORIAN ASSOCIATION

1910-1948

Published by the

PLAINCHANT PUBLICATIONS COMMITTEE

BASS VIEW, WEST FORTH STREET,
ANSTRUTHER, FIFE, SCOTLAND.

Printed in England

First Edition .	.	.	.	.	1916
Second Edition	.	.	.	.	1920
Third Edition .	.	.	.	.	1937
Fourth Edition	.	.	.	.	1946
Fifth Edition .	.	.	.	.	1951
Sixth Edition .	.	.	.	.	1955
Seventh Edition	.	.	.	.	1980

PRINTED IN GREAT BRITAIN BY
JOHN BLACKBURN LTD., OLD RUN ROAD, LEEDS LS10 2AA

INTRODUCTION

THE purpose of this publication is to further the singing of Plainsong in the English Church by setting out the most frequently used portion of the Prayer Book Psalter in a manner sufficiently simple to secure satisfactory results without the intervention of the Plainchant expert.

To this end the various pointing marks are few in number and more or less literary in character. In this connection the words of the late Archbishop Benson may, perhaps, be quoted. "I never can endure," wrote the Archbishop (*Life*, ii, p. 251) "to use a Psalter with notes to every syllable, or even elaborately pointed for singing. I feel, in spite of all I do, that the spirit vanishes from the words, and that I become as if I were chanting Vedas."

In the present work the most important addition to the text of the Psalter is the *accent-mark*. This is used persistently throughout the whole of every verse. It is introduced to safeguard the normal rhythm of the text, rather than to enforce any particular meaning which may be ascribed to any passage. For if the singers will only take care of the rhythm of the Psalms it may be left to theologians to teach us their meaning. In ordinary reading these accented syllables would be pronounced *more loudly* than the others. In singing, this emphasis is less pronounced, but it must not be allowed to disappear, for the preservation of the rhythmical beauty of the Psalter depends entirely upon the due observance of its accents. There must be no difference in treatment between the accents which appear

on the syllables sung to the reciting-note and those which occur
in the parts of the verse which are inflected.   In each case the
accented syllable must be *slightly emphasised*, but it is not thereby
lengthened, nor is the continuous flow of the text hindered.   The
only exception to this occurs when two accentuated syllables
come next to each other, as in

O Lórd, héal me,
and his náme pérish.

In such examples the first accented syllable will increase in
duration to about twice its normal length.   But these excep-
tional instances need not be specially looked for, nor should they
cause any anxiety either to the choir-master or to the singer, for
both in reading and in singing it is almost impossible to do
anything except the right thing when two accented syllables
fall together.

The *italicised syllable* in the text is that which takes the first
note of the inflexion.   It is not an indication of any change
of speed or of any alteration from the light, free style of
singing, which, it is hoped, will have preceded it.   In some
Tones the inflexion is usually begun on an accented syllable,
while in others the first of the inflected syllables may be
either strong or weak.   It will not be necessary to examine
the Tones analytically here, because the accent-mark will make
the precise treatment clear in every instance.   If the italicised
syllable is accented then it will receive the proper vocal stress,
as in Psalm vii, verse 12 :

Gód is a ríghteous Júdge, stróng and *pá*-tient :

If, on the other hand, the italicised syllable bears no accent-
mark it receives no emphasis of any kind.   Verses 13 and 14 of
Psalm vii are typical instances of inflection without accent :

he will whét *his* swórd :
the ínstruments *of* déath :

It is usually necessary to exercise great care to prevent the syllable immediately before the inflection being lengthened. Singers are apt to pause and pull themselves together before changing the note. This may be due to the bad tradition of regarding the change of note as the all-important factor upon which everything turns in psalmody, and the consequent anxiety to change at the right moment is usually the cause of hurried and jumbled singing in the earlier part of the verse. If, however, it is persistently made clear to the singers that the really important thing is the continual preservation of the verbal accentuation throughout every verse, the inflexion will become an incident instead of a feature, and will probably be accomplished quite naturally and easily.

The *tie-marks* which link certain syllables together are intended to show the precise method of treating every redundant syllable which may occur in the text. The treatment of an inflexion of four notes is simple when it is allied with four syllables, as in

a-bóve the héa-vens.

but when an additional syllable has to be included in such an inflexion for rhythmical reasons it sometimes takes the note of the previous syllable and sometimes that of the subsequent syllable. The position of the tie-mark indicates the exact treatment necessary. In Psalm viii the position of the tie-mark in the words

and to the Hó-ly⌒Ghóst.

indicates that the last two syllables have the same note. In Psalm xxxiii the corresponding passage is marked

and to the Hó⌒ly Ghóst.

indicating that both syllables of "Hó-ly" have the same note. Only one exception is made to this method of treating redundant syllables. In some of the Endings of Tone V it is customary to insert an intermediate *do* between the *ra* and *te* of the inflexion whenever an additional syllable intervenes, as will be seen in Psalm 136, as set out on page 117. There a tie-mark would not meet the case, for the redundant syllable has a note of its own. The expedient of underlining is therefore resorted to, and the syllable so underlined takes the interpolated note shown in brackets in the Tone at the head of the Psalm. In Psalm lxix, as set on page 141, such final syllables are underlined as return to the final note of the *Tonus in directum*.

The first two syllables of each Psalm are usually printed in CAPITALS. These syllables take the two notes or note-groups [termed the Intonation] which occur before the first reciting-note. In the Psalms only the first half of the first verse is so treated, but in the Gospel Canticles every verse is affected which has a sufficient number of syllables. Psalms liv, ci, cxxviii, cxxxi, and some of the sections of Psalm cxix, have no Intonations, but commence at once on the reciting-note, hence the first two syllables are not printed in capitals. Similarly, certain verses of the Gospel Canticles omit the Intonation in some Tones, and here again the absence of capitals will make this point quite clear. Attention must be drawn to Psalm cxiv, in which the Peregrine Tone has an Intonation in *each half* of the first verse, but nowhere else.

Very short Psalm-verses which omit any part of the inflexion are provided with short dashes which correspond with the omitted notes of the inflexion, the reciting-note being left out of account. When a half-verse begins at once with an italicised syllable, only the reciting-note is omitted. When the first note of the inflexion is also omitted, a dash replaces the corresponding (italicised) syllable. In verse 6 of Psalm cl the phrase

práise the⌐Lórd.

is sung to *ra* (*do*) *do*. These abbreviations have been reduced to a minimum, as Tones and Endings have generally been chosen with a view to avoiding them as much as possible.

Three punctuation marks are used in addition to the full-stop. The *colon* denotes the main division of the verse, as in the Book of Common Prayer. Musically it stands also for a pause or silence, the duration of which is dealt with hereafter. The *semi-colon* is used wherever the length or sense of a phrase demands a break for a short breath. The *comma* is retained according to the Prayer Book, and, although no break or breath is intended, it is essential that commas should not be ignored altogether, otherwise the recitation will sound mechanical and lifeless. The ideal manner of observing a comma is to retard very slightly the syllable which comes immediately before it, without making any break in the vocal tone. This retardation must never be exaggerated, but if it be reasonably and sensibly managed the commas will be found to convey through the ear the same rhythmical and rhetorical significance as is conveyed through the eye when they are read from the printed page.

A great deal of misapprehension exists as to the method of treating the concluding syllables of the half-verses. No absolutely uniform rule can be laid down either as to the nature and extent of the *rallantando* and *diminuendo* required, or as to the duration of the pause, or silence, at the colon. The disposition of the final accents, the number and excellence of the singers employed, the size and resonance of the building, are all factors which must be taken into account. In dealing with the conclusion of the half-verses it may be taken as a general rule that only the last rhythmic foot is subject to the softening-off and slowing-off process. That is to say, the normal speed is maintained until the last accented syllable is reached. If this happens to be the last syllable of all, as in

For Gód is my Kíng of óld :

only the final syllable should be lengthened, and it should only be softened off during that lengthening. Therefore the final syllable in the above example, being accented, should be begun firmly and emphatically, the subsequent *diminuendo* being

confined to the duration of the subsequent slight *rallantando*.
When the last rhythmic foot consists of one strong syllable and
one weak, as in

slåy the wick-ed:

both syllables take the *rallantando*, and the second syllable takes
the *diminuendo*. When the last rhythmic foot has three syllables,
as in

no pléasure in wick-ed⌒ness:

all three syllables take the *rallantando*, and the two last the
diminuendo. The duration of the pause at the colon should be
about equal to the duration of the last rhythmic foot immediately preceding it. This may appear to involve a silence varying
in length at the colon, but in practise it will be found that the
mental repetition of the preceding rhythmic foot is a very sure
and satisfactory means of obtaining absolute unanimity among
a body of singers.

The *dieresis* denotes that the syllable bearing it has two or
more notes alloted to it. Every syllable in the text without a
dieresis has only one note, therefore.

The method of pointing used in this Psalter is the outcome
of some twenty years work in teaching parish choirs to inflect
the Psalms freely and easily, and in accordance with the prin-
ciples first explained to the modern world by the Benedictines
of Solesmes. The Editor desires to express his indebtedness to
the Committee of the Gregorian Association for their kindness
in permitting him to use this system experimentally in their
annual service books until the method finally arrived at its
present form.

THE EVENING PSALMS

THE 1st EVENING

PSALM 6   *Domine ne in furore*   TONE II

O LÓRD, rebúke me nót in thine indig-*ná-*
tion : neither chásten me in thý *dis-*
pléa-sure.

2 Have mércy upon me, O Lórd, for I am
wéak : O Lórd, héal me, for my bónes *are* véx-ed.

3 My sóul also is sóre *tróu-*bled : but Lórd,
how lóng wilt *thou* pún⌐ish me ?

4 Túrn thee, O Lórd, and delíver my *sóul* : O
sáve me for *thy* mér⌐cies' sake.⸱

5 For in déath no man remémbereth *thée* : and
whó will give thee thánks *in* the pít ?

6 I am wéary of my gróaning ; évery níght wash
I my *béd* : and wáter my cóuch *with* my téars.

7 My béauty is góne for very *tróu-*ble : and
wórn awáy because of áll *mine* é⌐ne-mies.

8 Awáy from me, all yé that work *vá*-ni⌒ty : for the Lórd hath héard the voíce of *my* wéep-ing.

9 The Lórd hath héard my pe-*tí*-tion : the Lórd will *re*-ceíve⌒my prayer.

10 All mine énemies shall be confóunded, and sóre *véx*-ed : they shall be túrned báck, and put to *sháme* súd⌒den-ly.

Glóry be to the Fáther, and to the *Són* : and to *the* Hó⌒ly Ghost.

As it was in the begínning, is nów, and éver *sháll* be : wórld withóut *énd*.   A-men.

PSALM 7   *Domine Deus meus*   TONE I

O LÓRD my Gód, in thée have Í pút *my* trúst : sáve me from áll thém that pérse-cute me, *and* de-lĭ-ver⌒më.

2 Lést he devoúr my soúl, like a líon, and téar it in *píe*-ces : while *there* is nöne to⌒hëlp.

3 O Lórd my Gód, if I have done ány *such* thíng : or íf there be any wíck-*ed*-ness ĭn my⌒händs.

4 If I have rewárded évil unto him that dealt fríendly *with* me : yéa, I have delívered him that without ány cáuse *is* mine ë-ne⌒mÿ.

5 Then let mine énemy pérsecute my soúl, and *táke* me : yéa, let him tréad my lífe dówn upon the eárth ; and láy mine *hó*-nour ĭn the⌒düst.

6 Stánd up, O Lórd, in thy wráth ; and líft up thysélf, becáuse of the indignátion of mine é-*ne*-mies : aríse up for mé in the judgement which thóu *hast* com-män-dëd.

7 And so shall the congregátion of the péople cóme a-*bóut* thee : for theír sakes thérefore lift *up* thy-sëlf a⸗gaïn.

8 The Lórd shall júdge the péople ; give séntence with me, O Lórd : accórding to my ríghteousness ; and accórding to the ínnocency *that* is ïn më.

9 O let the wíckedness of the ungódly cóme to *an* énd : but *guíde* thou thë jüst.

10 For the rígh-*teous* Gód : tríeth the *vé*-ry hëarts and‸reïns.

11 My hélp cómeth éven *of* Gód : who presérveth thém *that* are trüe of‸hëart.

12 Gód is a ríghteous Júdge, stróng and *pá*-tient : and Gód is pro-*vók*-ed ëv-ery‸däy.

13 If a mán will not túrn, he will whét *his* swórd : he hath bént his bów and *made* it rëa-dÿ.

14 He hath prepáred for him the ínstruments *of* déath : he ordaíneth his árrows agaínst the *pér*-se-cü-törs.

15 Behóld, he trávaileth with *mis*-chief : he hath conceíved sórrow, and bróught *fórth* un-gödli⸗nëss.

16 He hath gráven and dígged up *a* pít : and is fállen himsélf into the destrúction that he *made* for öth-ër.

17 For his trávail shall cóme upon his *ówn* héad : and his wíckedness shall fáll *on* his öwn päte.

18 I will give thánks unto the Lórd, accórding to his rígh-*teous*-ness : and I will praíse the Náme *of* the Lörd most‿Hïgh.

Glóry be to the Fáther, and to *the* Són : and *to* the Hö-ly‿Ghöst.

As it was in the begínning, is nów, and éver *sháll* be : wórld with-*óut* énd. Ä-mën.

PSALM 8   *Domine Dominus noster*   TONE VIII

O LÓRD our Góvernour, how éxcellent is thy Náme in áll the *wórld* : thou that hast sét thy glóry a-*bóve* the héa-vens.

2 Out of the móuth of very bábes and súcklings hast thou ordáined stréngth, becáuse of thine *é*-ne⁼mies : that thou mightest stíll the énemy, and *the* a-vén-ger.

3 For, I will consíder thy héavens, éven the wórks of thy *fín*-gers : the móon and the stárs, which thóu *hast* or-daín-ed.

4 Whát is mán that thou art míndful of *hím* : and the són of mán, that thou *ví*-si-test hím ?

5 Thou mádest him lówer than the *án*-gels : to crówn him with gló-*ry* and wór-ship.

6 Thou mákest him to háve domínion óver the

wórks of thy *hánds* : and thóu hast put áll thíngs in subjéction *ún*-der his féet.

7 'All shéep and *óx*-en : yéa, and the *béasts* of the fíeld.

8 The fówls of the aír, and the físhes of the *séa* : and whátsoever wálketh through the *páths* of the séas.

9 O Lórd our *Gó*-ver͡nour : how éxcellent is thy *Náme* in áll the͡wórld.

Glóry be to the Fáther, and to the *Són* : and *to* the Hó-ly͡Ghóst.

As it wás in the begínning, is nów, and éver *sháll* be : wórld with-*óut* énd.   A-men.

THE 2nd EVENING

PSALM 12   *Salvum me fac*   TONE IV

HÉLP ME, Lórd, for thére is not óne gód-*ly* mán léft : for the faíthful are mínished from amóng *the* chíl-dren of mén.

2 They tálk of vánity évery one *with* his neígh-bour : they dó but flátter with their líps, and dissém-*ble* in their dóu͡ble héart.

3 The Lórd shall róot out áll de-*ceit*-ful líps : and the tóngue *that* spéak-eth próud thíngs ;

4 Whích have saíd, With our tóngue will *wé* pre-

vaíl : wé are théy that óught to spéak ; *whó* is
lórd ó͡ver us ?

5 Nów for the cómfortless tróubles' sáke *of*
the née-dy : and becáuse of the *déep* sígh-ing
of^the póor,

6 I will úp, *saith* the Lórd : and will hélp évery
óne from hím that swélleth agaínst him, and *will*
sét him at rést.

7 The wórds of the Lórd *are* púre wórds : éven
as the sílver, which from the éarth is tríed ; and
púrified *sé*-ven tímes in^the fíre.

8 Thóu shalt kéep *them*, O Lórd : thóu shalt
presérve him from thís gene-*rá*-tion for év-er.

9 The ungódly wálk on *év*-ery síde : whén they
are exálted, the chíldren of *mén* are pút to^re-
-búke.

Glóry be to the Fáther, and *to* the Són : *and*
to the Hó͡ly Ghóst.

As it wás in the begínning, is nów, and *év*-er
sháll be : wórld *with*-óut énd. A-men.

PSALM 13   *Usque quo Domine*   TONE V

H OW LONG wilt thóu forgét me, O Lord,
for *év*-er : how lóng wilt thou *hide* thy
fáce^from më ?

2 How lóng shall I séek cóunsel in my sóul, and

be so véxed in my *heart* : how lóng shall mine
énemies *tri*-umph ó⌣ver më ?

3 Consíder, and héar me, O Lórd my *Gód* :
líghten mine éyes, that I *sléep* not in dëath.

4 Lést mine énemy sáy, I have preváiled a-*gaínst*
him : for íf I be cást dówn, théy that tróuble me
will re-joíce⌣at ït.

5 But my trúst is in thy *mér*-cy : and my héart
is jóyful in *thy* sal-vá-tïon.

6 I will síng of the Lórd, becáuse he hath déalt
so lóvingly *with* me : yéa, I will praíse the Náme
of the *Lórd* most Hígh-ëst.

Glóry be to the Fáther, and to the *Són* : and
to the Hó⌣ly Ghöst.

As it wás in the begínning, is nów, and éver
shall be : wórld with-*óut* énd.   A-mën.

PSALM 14   *Dixit insipiens*   TONE VI

THE FÓOL hath *said* in his héart : *Thére*
ïs nó Gód.

2 Théy are corrúpt, and becóme abóminable *in*
their dó-ings : thére is nóne that dó-*eth* göod,
nó not⌣óne.

3 The Lórd lóoked dówn from héaven upón
the *chíl*-dren of mén : to sée if there were ány
that would únderstánd * nd* sëek áf-ter⌣Gód.

4 But théy are áll gone óut of the wáy; théy are áltógether becóme a-*bó*-mi-na-ble : thére is nóne that dó-*eth* göod, nó not^óne.

5 Their thróat is an ópen sépulchre, with their tóngues have *théy* de-ceív-ed : the poíson of ásps is *ún*-dër their líps.

6 Their móuth is fúll of *cúrs*-ing^and bít°ter--ness : their féet are *swíft* tö shéd blóod.

7 Destrúction and unháppiness is ín their wáys, and the wáy of péace *have* they nót knówn : thére is no féar of *Gód* bë-fóre their^éyes.

8 Háve they no knówledge, that théy are áll such *wórk*-ers^of mís-chief : eáting up my péople as it wére bréad, and cáll *not* üp-ón the^Lórd ?

9 Thére were they bróught in gréat féar, éven *where* no féar was : for Gód is in the generátion *of* thë rígh-teous.

10 As for yóu, ye have máde a móck at the *cóun*-sel of^the póor : becáuse he pútteth *his* trüst in the^Lórd.

11 Whó shall gíve salvátion unto Ísrael out of Sýon ? When the Lórd túrneth the captívity *of* his péo-ple : thén shall Jácob rejoíce, and Ís-*ra*-ël sháll be^glád.

Glóry be to the *Fá*-ther,^and to^the Són : and *to* thë Hó-ly^Ghóst.

As it wás in the begínning, is nów, and *év*-er sháll be : wórld with-*óut* ënd. A-men.

THE 3rd EVENING

PSALM 18   *Diligam te Domine*   TONE VIII

I WILL lóve thee, O Lórd, my stréngth ; the Lórd is my stóny róck, and mý de-*fénce* : my Sáviour, my Gód, and my míght, in whóm I will trúst ; my búckler, the hórn álso of mý salvátion, *and* my ré-fuge.

2 I will cáll upón the Lórd, which is wórthy to be *prái*-sed : só shall I be sáfe *from* mine é-ne-mies.

3 The sórrows of déath cómpassed *mé* : and the óverflówings of ungódliness *máde* me a-fráid.

4 The paíns of héll came a-*bóut* me : the snáres of déath *o*-ver-tóok me.

5 In my tróuble I will cáll upon the *Lórd* : and compláin *un*-to mý Gód.

6 Só shall he héar my voíce out of his hóly *tém*-ple : and my cómplaint shall cóme befóre him ; it shall énter éven *in*-to hís éars.

7 The éarth trémbled and *quá*-ked : the véry foundátions álso of the hílls shóok, and were remóved, be-*cáuse* he was wróth.

8 There wént a smóke óut in his *pré*-sence : and a consúming fíre óut of his móuth, so that cóals were *kín*-dled at it.

A

9 He bówed the héavens álso, and cáme *dówn* : and it was dárk *ún*-der his féet.

10 He róde upón the chérubims, and did *flý* : he came flýing upón the *wings* of the wínd.

11 He máde dárkness his sécret *pláce* : his pavílion róund abóut him; with dárk wáter, and thíck *clóuds* to cóv-er^him.

12 At the bríghtness of his présence his clóuds re-*mó*-ved : haíl-*stónes*, and cóals of^fíre.

13 The Lórd also thúndered out of héaven, and the Híghest gáve his *thún*-der : haíl-*stónes*, and cóals of^fíre.

14 He sént out his árrows, and scáttered *them* : he cást forth líghtnings, *and* de-stróy-ed^them.

15 The spríngs of wáters were séen ; and the foundátions of the róund wórld were discóvered, at thy chíding, O *Lórd* : at the blásting of the bréath of *thý* dis-pléa-sure.

16 Hé shall sénd dówn from on hígh to *fétch* me : and shall táke me óut of *má*-ny wá-ters.

17 Hé shall delíver me from my stróngest énemy, and from thém which *háte* me : for théy are too *migh*-ty for me.

18 They prevénted me in the dáy of my *tróu*-ble : but the Lórd was *mý* up-hóld-er.

19 He bróught me fórth álso into a pláce of *li*-ber²ty : he bróught me fórth, éven becáuse he hád a *fá*-vour ún-to^me.

20 The Lórd shall rewárd me áfter my ríghteous

déal-ing : accórding to the cléanness of my hánds shall he *ré*-com-pense me.

21 Becáuse I have képt the wáys of the *Lórd* : and have nót forsáken my Gód, *as* the wíck-
-ed^dóth.

22 For Í have an éye unto áll his *láws* : and will nót cast óut his com-*mánd*-ments fróm me.

23 I was álso uncorrúpt be-*fóre* him : and eschéwed *mine* own wíck-ed^ness.

24 Thérefore shall the Lórd rewárd me áfter my ríghteous *déal*-ing : and accórding unto the cléanness of my hánds *in* his éye-sight.

25 With the hóly thou shált be *hó*-ly : and with a pérfect mán thou *shált* be pér-fect.

26 With the cléan thou shált be *cléan* : and with the fróward thou *shalt* léarn fró-ward^ness.

27 For thóu shalt sáve the péople that are ín ad-*vér*-si^ty : and shalt bríng dówn the *hígh* lóoks of the^próud.

28 Thou álso shalt líght my *cán*-dle : the Lórd my Gód shall máke my *dárk*-ness to be^líght.

29 For in thée I shall discómfit an hóst of *mén* : and with the hélp of my Gód I shall léap ó-ver the wáll.

30 The wáy of Gód is an úndefíled *wáy* : the wórd of the Lórd álso is tríed in the fíre ; hé is the defénder of all thém that *pút* their trúst in^hím.

31 For whó is Gód, but the *Lórd* : or whó hath ány *stréngth*, ex-cépt our^Gód ?

32 It is Gód, that gírdeth me with stréngth of
wár : and máketh *my* wáy pér-fect.

33 He máketh my féet like *hárts'* feet : and
sét-*teth* me úp on^hígh.

34 He téacheth mine hánds to *fíght* : and mine
árms shall bréak é-*ven* a bów of^stéel.

35 Thóu hast gíven me the defénce of thý
sal-*vá*-tion : thy ríght hand álso shall hóld me
úp ; and thy lóving corréc-*tion* shall máke me^gréat.

36 Thóu shalt make róom enough únder me fór
to *gó* : that my *fóot*-steps sháll not^slíde.

37 I will fóllow upon mine énemies, and óver-
-*táke* them : neíther will I túrn agaín till I *háve*
de-stróy-ed^thém.

38 I will smíte them, that théy shall nót be áble
to *stánd* : but fáll *un*-der mý féet.

39 Thou hast gírded me with stréngth únto the
bát-tle : thou shalt thrów dówn mine é-*ne*-mies
ún-der^me.

40 Thou hast máde mine énemies álso to túrn
their bácks up-*ón* me : and I shall destróy *them*
that háte me.

41 They shall crý, but there shall be nóne to
hélp them : yéa, éven unto the Lórd shall they
crý, but he *sháll* not héar them.

42 I will béat them as smáll as the dúst befóre
the *wínd* : I will cást them óut as the *cláy* in
the stréets.

43 Thou shalt delíver me from the strívings of

the *péo*-ple : and thóu shalt máke me the héad
of the héa-then.

44 A péople whom I háve not *knówn* : — shall
sérve me.

45 As sóon as they héar of me, théy shall o-*béy*
me : but the stránge chíldren shall dis-*sém*-ble
wíth me.

46 The stránge chíldren shall *fail* : and be
afraíd óut *of* their prí-sons.

47 The Lórd líveth, and bléssed be my stróng
hél-per : and praísed be the Gód of *my* sal-vá-tion.

48 'Even the Gód that séeth that I be a-*vén*-ged :
and subdúeth the *péo*-ple ún-to^me.

49 It is hé that delívereth me from my crúel
énemies ; and sétteth me úp abóve mine
ádver-*sa*-ries : thóu shalt ríd me *fróm* the
wíc-ked^mán.

50 For thís caúse will I give thánks unto thée,
O Lórd, amóng the *Gén*-tiles : and sing praíses
ún-to thy Náme.

51 Gréat prospérity gíveth he únto his *Kíng* :
and shéweth lóving-kíndness unto Dávid his
Anoínted ; and únto his *séed* for év-er^more.

Glóry be to the Fáther, and to the *Són* : and
to the Hó-ly^Ghóst.

As it wás in the begínning, is nów, and éver
sháll be : wórld with-*óut* énd.   A-men.

THE 4th EVENING

PSALM 22   *Deus Deus meus*   TONE IV

MY GÓD, my Gód, lóok upón me ; whý
hast *thóu* for-sák-en^me : and árt so fár
from my héalth, and from the wórds of mý
com-*plaint* ?

2 O my Gód, I crý in the dáy-time, but thou
héar-est nót : and in the níght-séason álso I táke
no *rést*.

3 And thóu contín-*u*-est hó-ly : O thou wórship
of 'Isra-*el*.

4 Our fáthers hóp-*ed* in thée : they trústed in
thée, and thou dídst delíver *them*.

5 They cálled upon thée, *and* were hól-pen :
they pút their trúst in thée, and were nót con-
fóund-*ed*.

6 But ás for mé, I am a wórm, *and* nó mán :
a véry scórn of mén, and the óutcast of the
péo-*ple*.

7 'All they that sée me láugh *me* to scórn : they
shóot out their líps, and sháke their héads,
sáy-*ing*,

8 He trústed in Gód, that hé *would* de-lív-
-er^him : lét him delíver him, if hé will háve *him*.

9 But thóu art hé that tóok me óut of my

mó-ther's wómb : thóu wast my hópe, when I hánged yét upón my móther's *bréasts*.

10 I have been léft unto thée éver since *I* was bórn : thóu art my Gód éven from my móther's *wómb*.

11 O gó not fróm me, for tróuble is *hárd* at hánd : and thére is nóne to hélp *me*.

12 Mány óxen are *cóme* a-bóut me : fát búlls of Básan clóse me ín on évery *side*.

13 They gápe upón me *with* their móuths : as it were a rámping and a róaring lí-*on*.

14 I am póured out like wáter, and áll my bónes are *óut* of joínt : my héart álso in the mídst of my bódy is éven like mélting *wáx*.

15 My stréngth is dríed úp like a pótsherd ; and my tóngue cléaveth *to* my gúms : and thóu shalt bríng me ínto the dúst of *déath*.

16 For mány dógs are *cóme* a-bóut me : and the cóuncil of the wícked láyeth síege agaínst *me*.

17 They píerced my hánds and my féet ; I may téll *all* my bónes : they stánd stáring and lóoking upón *me*.

18 They párt my gár-*ments* a-móng them : and cást lóts upon my vés-*ture*.

19 But bé not thou fár from *mé*, O Lórd : thóu art my súccour, háste thee to hélp *me*.

20 Delíver my sóul *from* the swórd : my dárling from the pówer of the *dóg*.

21 Sáve me from the *li*-on's móuth : thou hast

héard me álso from amóng the hórns of the
úni-*corns*.

22 I will decláre thy Náme ún-*to* my bré-thren :
in the mídst of the cóngregátion will I praíse
thee.

23 O praíse the Lórd, *ye* that féar him : mágnify
him, áll yé of the séed of Jácob ; and féar him,
áll ye séed of 'Isra-*el* ;

24 For he hath nót despísed, nor abhórred, the
lów estáte *of* the póor : he hath nót híd his fáce
from hím ; but whén he cálled unto hím he
héard *him*.

25 My praíse is of thée in the gréat *con*-gre-
-gá-tion : my vóws will I perfórm in the síght of
thém that féar *him*.

26 The póor shall éat, and be *sá*-tis-fi-ed : théy
that séek áfter the Lórd shall práise him ; your
héart shall líve for év-*er*.

27 'All the énds of the wórld shall remémber
themselves ; and be túrned ún-*to* the Lórd :
and áll the kíndreds of the nátions shall wórship
befóre *him*.

28 For the kíngdom *is* the Lórd's : and hé is the
Góvernour amóng the péo-*ple*.

29 All súch as be fát *up*-on éarth : have éaten,
and wórship-*ped*.

30 All théy that go dówn into the dúst shall
knéel be-fóre him : and nó mán hath quíckened
his ówn *sóul*.

31 My *séed* shall sérve him : they shall be cóunted
unto the Lórd for a generá-*tion*.

32 Théy shall cóme, and the héavens shall
de-*cláre* his rígh-teous^ness : únto a péople that
sháll be bórn, whóm the Lórd hath *máde.*

Glóry be to the Fáther, and *to* the Són : and
to the Hóly *Ghóst.*

As it wás in the begínning, is nów, and *év*-er
sháll be : wórld withóut énd. A-*men.*

Psalm 23   *Dominus regit me*   Tone VIII

THE LÓRD is my *shép*-herd : thérefore can
I lack nó-thĭng.

2 Hé shall féed me in a gréen *pás*-ture : and
léad me fórth besíde the wá-*ters* of cóm-fört.

3 Hé shall convért my *sóul* : and bríng me fórth
in the páths of ríghteousness, *for* his Náme's säke.

4 Yéa, though I wálk through the válley of the
shádow of déath, I will féar no *é*-vil : for thóu
art wíth me ; thy ród and *thy* stáff cóm-fort^më.

5 Thóu shalt prepáre a táble befóre me against
thém that *tróu*-ble^me : thóu hast anóinted my
héad with oíl, and my *cúp* shall be füll.

6 But thy lóving-kíndness and mércy shall
fóllow me áll the dáys of my *lífe* : and I will
dwéll in the hóuse of the *Lórd* for év-ër.

Glóry be to the Fáther, and to the *Són* : and
to the Hó-ly^Ghöst.

As it wás in the begínning, is nów, and ever
sháll be : wórld with-*óut* énd. A-mën.

THE 5th EVENING

PSALM 27   *Dominus illuminatio*   TONE I

THE LÓRD is my líght, and my salvátion;
whóm thén shall *I* féar : the Lórd is the
stréngth of my lífe; of whóm then *sháll* I
be^a-fraïd ?

2 When the wícked, éven mine énemies, and
my fóes, came upón me to éat up *my* flésh : they
stúm-bled and fëll.

3 Thóugh an hóst of mén were laíd agaínst me,
yét shall nót my héart be *a*-fraíd : and thóugh
there róse up wár agaínst me, yét will I *pút* my
trúst^in hīm.

4 'One thing have I desíred of the Lórd, which
I wíll *re*-quíre : éven that I may dwéll in the
hóuse of the Lórd áll the dáys of my lífe; to
behóld the faír béauty of the Lórd, and to ví-*sit*
his tém-plë.

5 For in the tíme of tróuble he shall híde me
in his táber-*na*-cle : yéa, in the sécret pláce of his
dwélling shall he híde me; and sét me úp up-*ón*
a róck^of stöne.

6 And nów shall he líft up *mine* héad : abóve
mine énemies *róund* a-bóut më.

7 Thérefore will I óffer in his dwélling **an**

oblátion with gréat *glád*-ness : I will síng, and spéak praíses *un*-to the Lörd.

8 Héarken unto my voíce, O Lórd, when I cry un-*to* thée : have mércy upón *me*, and héar më.

9 My héart hath tálked of thée ; Séek ye *my* fáce : Thy fáce, *Lórd*, will I sëek.

10 O híde not thóu thy fáce *from* mé : nor cást thy sérvant awáy *in* dis-pléa-süre.

11 Thóu hast béen my *súc*-cour : léave me nót, neíther forsáke me, O Gód of *my* sal-vá-tīon.

12 When my fáther and my móther for-*sáke* me : the Lórd *tá*-keth me üp.

13 Téach me thy wáy, O Lórd : and léad me in the ríght wáy, becáuse *of* mine én᷍e-mīes.

14 Delíver me not óver ínto the wíll of mine ádver-*sa*-ries : for thére are fálse wítnesses rísen up agaínst me, and *súch* as spéak wröng.

15 I should útterly have *faínt*-ed : but that I belíeve vérily to sée the góodness of the Lórd in the lánd *of* the lív-īng.

16 O tárry thóu the Lórd's *lei*-sure : be stróng, and hé shall cómfort thine héart ; and put thóu thy *trúst* in the Lörd.

Glóry be to the Fáther, and to *the* Són : and *to* the Hó᷍ly Ghöst.

As it wás in the begínning, is nów, and éver *shall* be : wórld with-*óut* énd. A-mën.

UNTO thée will I crý, O *Lórd*, my stréngth :
think no scórn of me ; lést, if thou máke
as thóugh thou héarest nót, I becóme like thém
that *go* dówn in-to the⌢pít.

2 Héar the voíce of my húmble petítions, when
I crý *un*-to thée : when I hóld up my hánds
towárds the mércy-séat of *thy* hó-ly tém-ple.

3 O plúck me nót awáy, neíther destróy me
with the ungódly and *wíck*-ed dó-ers : which
spéak fríendly to their neíghbours ; but imágine
mís-chief in their héarts.

4 Rewárd them accórding *to* their déeds : and
accórding to the wíckedness of *their* ówn in-
-vén-tions.

5 Récompense them áfter the wórk *of* their
hánds : páy them thát *they* háve de-sérv-ed.

6 For théy regárd nót in their mínd the wórks
of the Lórd, nor the operátion *of* his hánds :
thérefore sháll he bréak them *dówn*, and not
buíld them⌢úp.

7 Praísed *be* the Lórd : for hé hath héard the
voíce of my *húm*-ble pe-tí-tions.

8 The Lórd is my stréngth, and my shíeld ;
my héart hath trústed in hím, and *I* am hélp-ed :
thérefore my héart dánceth for jóy ; and ín my
sóng will I praíse him.

9 The Lórd *is* mý stréngth : and hé is the
whólesome defénce *of* his An-oínt-ed.

10 O sáve thy péople, and gíve thy bléssing unto
thíne in-hé-ri-tance : féed them, and sét *them* úp
for év-er.

Glóry be to the Fáther, and *to* the Són : *and*
to the Hó-ly Ghóst.

As it wás in the begínning, is nów, and *év*-er
sháll be : wórld *with*-óut énd.   A-men.

PSALM 29   *Afferte Domino*   TONE VIII

BRING UN-to the Lórd, O ye míghty ; bríng
young ráms unto the *Lórd* : ascríbe unto
the Lórd *wór*-ship and stréngth.

2 Gíve the Lórd the hónour dúe unto his
Náme : wórship the Lórd with *hó*-ly wór-ship.

3 It is the Lórd, that commándeth the *wá*-ters :
it is the glórious Gód, that mák-*eth* the thún-der.

4 It is the Lórd, that rúleth the séa ; the voíce
of the Lórd is míghty in ope-*rá*-tion : the voíce
of the Lórd is a *gló*-ri-ous voíce.

5 The voíce of the Lórd bréaketh the *cé*-
-dar-trées : yéa, the Lórd bréaketh the cé-*dars*
of Lí-ba-nus.

6 He máketh them álso to skíp like a *cálf* :
Líbanus álso, and Sírion, líke *a* young ú-ni-corn.

7 The voíce of the Lórd divídeth the flámes

of fíre ; the voíce of the Lórd sháketh the
wíl-der꞉ness : yéa, the Lórd sháketh the wílder-
ness of Cá-des.

8 The voíce of the Lórd máketh the hínds
to bríng forth yóung; and discóvereth the thíck
búsh-es : in his témple doth évery man spéak *of*
his hó-nour.

9 The Lórd sítteth abóve the *wá*-ter꞉flóod :
and the Lórd remaíneth a *Kíng* for év-er.

10 The Lórd shall give stréngth unto his *péo*-ple :
the Lórd shall gíve his péople the *blés*-sing of
péace.

Glóry be to the Fáther, and to the *Són* : and
to the Hó-ly⌒Ghóst.

As it wás in the begínning, is nów, and éver
sháll be : wórld with-*óut* énd.   A-men.

THE   6th   EVENING

PSALM 32   *Beati quorum*   TONE V

BLÉSSED is hé whose unríghteousness is
for-*gív*-en : and whose *sín* is có-ver꞉ed.

2 Bléssed is the mán unto whóm the Lórd
impúteth nó *sín* : and in whóse spírit *there* is nó
guíle.

3 For whíle I héld my *tóngue* : my bónes
consúmed awáy through my *daí*-ly com-plaín-ing.

4 For thy hánd is heávy upón me dáy and *níght* : and my moísture is líke the *dróught* in súm-mer.

5 I will acknówledge my sín únto *thée* : and míne unríghteousness *háve* I nót híd.

6 I saíd, I will conféss my síns únto the *Lórd* : and só thou forgávest the *wíck-ed*-ness of my⌒sín.

7 For thís shall évery óne that is gódly máke his práyer unto thée; in a tíme when thou máyest be *fóund* : but in the gréat wáter-floods théy shall *nót* come nígh hím.

8 Thóu art a pláce to híde me in ; thóu shalt presérve me from *tróu*-ble : thou shalt cómpass me abóut with *sóngs* of de-lí-ver⌐ance.

9 I will infórm thee, and téach thee in the wáy whérein thóu shalt *gó* : and I will *guíde* thee wíth mine⌒éye.

10 Bé ye nót like to hórse and múle, which háve no únder-*stánd*-ing : whose móuths must be héld with bít and brídle, lést they *fáll* up-ón thee.

11 Gréat plágues remaín for the un-*gód*-ly : but whóso pútteth his trúst in the Lórd; mércy embráceth *hím* on év-ery⌐síde.

12 Be glád, O ye ríghteous, and rejoíce in the *Lórd* : and be jóyful, all *yé* that are trúe of⌒héart.

Glóry be to the Fáther, and to the *Són* : and *to* the Hó-ly⌒Ghóst.

As it wás in the begínning, is nów, and éver *sháll* be : wórld with-*óut* énd.   A-men.

R EJŌICE in the Lórd, *O* ye rígh-teous : for
it becómeth wéll the júst *to* be thánk-fül.

2 *Praise* the Lórd⁀with hárp : síng práises únto
hím with the lúte, and ínstru-*ment* of tén strĭngs.

3 Síng unto the *Lórd* a néw sóng : sing práises
lústily unto hím *with* a⁀góod cóur-äge.

4 For the *wórd* of⁀the Lórd⁀is trúe : and áll his
wórks are faíth-fül.

5 He lóveth ríghteous-*ness* and júdge-ment : the
éarth is fúll of the *góod*-ness of⁀the Lörd.

6 By the wórd of the *Lórd* were⁀the héa⁀vens
máde : and áll the hósts of them by the *bréath*
of his möuth.

7 He gáthereth the wáters of the séa togéther,
as it *wére* up-ón⁀an héap : and láyeth up the
déep, as *in* a tréa⁀sure-höuse.

8 Let áll the *éarth* féar the Lórd : stánd in áwe
of him, all yé that *dwéll* in the wörld.

9 For he *spáke*, and it⁀was dóne : he commánded, *and* it stóod fäst.

10 The Lórd bríngeth the cóunsel of the
héa-then to nóught : and máketh the devíces of
the péople to be of nóne efféct ; and cásteth óut
the *cóun*-sels⁀of prín-cës.

11 The cóunsel of the Lórd shall en-*dúre* for
év-er : and the thóughts of his héart from
géneratión to *gé*-ne-rá-tĭon.

12 Bléssed are the péople, whose Gód is the *Lórd* Je-hó-vah : and bléssed are the fólk, that he hath chósen to hím to be *his* in-hé⌒ri-tänce.

13 The Lórd looked dówn from héaven, and behéld áll the *chíl*-dren of mén : from the habitátion of his dwélling he consídereth all thém that *dwéll* on the ëarth.

14 He fáshioneth *all* the héarts⌒of thém : and únder-*stánd*-eth áll⌒their wörks.

15 Thére is nó kíng that can be sáved by the *múl*-ti⌒tude of⌒an hóst : neíther is ány míghty mán delíver-*ed* by múch strëngth.

16 A hórse is cóunted but a vaín *thing* to sáve⌒a mán : neíther shall he delíver ány man *by* his gréat strëngth.

17 Behóld, the éye of the Lórd is upon *thém* that féar him : and upon thém that pút their trúst *in* his mér-̈cÿ ;

18 To de-*lí*-ver⌒their sóul⌒from déath : and to féed them *in* the tíme⌒of dëarth.,

19 Our sóul hath pátiently *tár*-ried for⌒the Lórd : for hé is our *hélp*, and óur shïeld.

20 For our *héart* shall⌒re-joíce⌒in hím : becáuse we have hóped *in* his hó⌒ly Näme.

21 Lét thy mérciful kíndness, O Lórd, *be* up-ón us : líke as wé do *pút* our trúst⌒in thëe.

Glóry be to the *Fá*-ther,⌒and to⌒the Són : and *to* the Hó⌒ly Ghöst.

As it wás in the begínning, is nów, and *év*-er sháll be : wórld with-*óut* énd.   A-mën.

PSALM 34   *Benedicam Domino*   TONE III

I WILL álway give *thánks* un⌐to the Lórd :
his praíse shall év-*er* be in mý móuth.

2 My sóul shall máke her *bóast* in the Lórd :
the húmble shall héar *there*-of, and be glád.

3 O *praíse* the^Lórd with mé : and let us
mágnify *his* Náme to-géth-er.

4 I soúght the *Lórd*, and^he héard me : yéa,
he delívered *me* óut of áll my^féar.

5 They hád an éye unto hím, *and* were^líght-
-en-ed : and their fáces *were* nót a-shám-ed.

6 Ló, the póor críeth, and the *Lórd* héar-eth
hím : yéa, and sáveth him óut *of* áll his tróu-bles.

7 The ángel of the Lórd tárrieth round about
thém that féar him : and *de*-lí-ver-eth thém.

8 O táste, and sée, how *grá*-cious^the Lórd is :
bléssed is the mán *that* trúst-eth in hím.

9 O féar the Lórd, *yé* that^are his saínts : for
théy that *féar* him lack nó-thing.

10 The líons do láck, and *súf*-fer hún-ger : but
théy who séek the Lórd shall wánt no mánner
of thíng that is góod.

11 Cóme, ye chíldren, and *héark*-en^ún-to mé :
I will téach you *the* féar of the Lórd.

12 Whát mán is hé that *lúst*-eth to líve : and
would faín see góod dáys ?

13 Kéep thy *tóngue* from é-vil : and thy *lĩps*, that they spéak no^guíle.

14 Eschéw *é*-vil,^and dó góod : séek *péace*, and en-súe it.

15 The éyes of the Lórd are *ó*-ver^the rígh-teous : and his éars are ó-*pen* ún-to theír práyers.

16 The cóuntenance of the Lórd is agaínst thém *that* do é-vil : to róot óut the remém-*brance* of them fróm the^eárth.

17 The ríghteous crý, and the *Lórd* héar-eth thém : and delívereth them óut *of* áll their tróu-bles.

18 The Lórd is nígh unto thém that are *of* a^cón-trite héart : and will sáve súch as be of̱ *an* húm-ble spí-rit.

19 Gréat are the tróubles *of* the ríght-eous : but the Lórd delí-*ver*-eth him óut of^áll.

20 He *kéep*-eth^áll his bónes : so that not óne *of* thém is bró-ken.

21 But misfórtune shall *sláy* the^un-gód-ly : and théy that háte the rígh-*teous* shall be dé-so∗late.

22 The Lórd delívereth the *sóuls* of^his sér-vants : and áll théy that pút their trúst in hím *shall* nót be dé-sti∗tute.

Glóry be to the *Fá*-ther,^and^to the Són : *and* to the Hó-ly^Ghóst.

As it wás in the begínning, is nów, and *év*-er shall be : wórld *with*-óut énd.   A-men.

THE 7th EVENING

PSALM 37   *Noli œmulari*   TONE I

F RÉT NOT thysélf becáuse of the un-*gód*-ly :
neíther be thou énvious against the *é*-vil
dó-ers.

2 For théy shall sóon be cút dówn like *the*
gráss : and be wíthered éven *as* the gréen hérb.

3 Put thóu thy trúst in the Lórd, and be
dó-*ing* góod : dwéll in the lánd, and vérily *thou*
shalt be féd.

4 Delíght thou ín *the* Lórd : and hé shall gíve
thee thy héart's de⌒síre.

5 Commít thy wáy unto the Lórd, and pút
thy trúst *in* hím : and hé shall *bríng* it to páss.

6 He shall máke thy ríghteousness as cléar as
the líght : and thy júst déaling *as* the nóon-dáy.

7 Hóld thee stíll in the Lórd, and abíde
pátiently up-*ón* hím : but gríeve not thysélf
at hím whose wáy doth prósper ; against the
mán that dóeth after *é*-vil cóun-sels.

8 Léave óff from wráth, and lét gó dis-*pléa*-
sure : frét not thysélf, élse shalt thóu be móved
to dó é-vil.

9 Wícked dóers shall be róot-*ed* óut : and théy
that pátiently abíde the Lórd, thóse shall
in-*hé*-rit the lánd.

10 Yét a líttle whíle, and the ungódly shall be *cléan* góne : thóu shalt look áfter his pláce, and *hé* shall be a⌒wáy.

11 But the méek-spírited shall posséss *the* eárth : and shall be refréshed in the *múl*-ti-tude of⌒peáce.

12 The ungódly séeketh cóunsel agaínst *the* júst : and gnásheth up-*ón* him wíth his⌒téeth.

13 The Lórd shall láugh him *to* scórn : for he hath séen that his *dáy* is cóm-ing.

14 The ungódly have dráwn out the swórd, and have bént *their* bów : to cást dówn the póor and néedy ; and to sláy súch as are of a ríght *con*-ver-sá-tion.

15 Their swórd shall gó thróugh their *ówn* héart : and their bów *shall* be bró-ken.

16 A smáll thíng that the rígh-*teous* hath : is bétter than gréat ríches of *the* un-gód-ly.

17 For the árms of the ungódly shall be *bró*-ken : and the Lórd uphóld-*eth* the rígh-teous.

18 The Lórd knóweth the dáys of the *gód*-ly : and their inhéritance shall en-*dúre* for év-er.

19 They shall nót be confóunded in the péri-*lous* tíme : and in the dáys of déarth *they* shall háve e⌒nóugh.

20 As for the ungódly, they shall pérish ; and the énemies of the Lórd shall consúme as the fát *of* lámbs : yéa, even as the smóke, shall *théy* con-súme a⌒wáy.

21 The ungódly bórroweth, and páyeth not

á-gaín : but the ríghteous is mérci-*ful*, and
lí-be⌐ral.

22 Súch as are bléssed of Gód shall posséss *the*
lánd : and théy that are cúrsed of hím *shall* be
róot-ed^óut.

23 The Lórd órdereth a góod man's *gó*-ing : and
máketh his wáy accép-*ta*-ble to him⌐sélf.

24 Thóugh he fáll, he shall nót be cást *a*-wáy :
for the Lórd uphóld-*eth* him with his^hánd.

25 I have been yóung, and nów *am* óld : and
yét saw I néver the ríghteous forsáken; nor his
séed *bég*-ging their bréad.

26 The ríghteous is éver mérciful, and *lénd*-eth :
and his *séed* is blés-sed.

27 Flée from évil, and dó the thíng that *is*
góod : and *dwéll* for év-er⌐more.

28 For the Lórd lóveth the thíng that *is* ríght :
he forsáketh not hís that be gódly ; but they
are presérv-*ed* for év-er.

29 The unríghteous sháll be pún-*ish*-ed : ás
for the séed of the ungódly, ít *shall* be róot-ed^oút.

30 The ríghteous shall inhérit *the* lánd : and
dwéll there-*ín* for év-er.

31 The móuth of the ríghteous is éxercised in
wís-dom : and his tóngue will be tálk-*ing* of
júdge-ment.

32 The láw of his Gód is ín *his* héart : and his
gó-ings sháll not^slíde.

33 The ungódly séeth the *rígh*-teous : and
séeketh occá-*sion* to sláy hím.

34 The Lórd will not léave him in *his* hánd :
nor condémn him whén *he* is júdg-ed.

35 Hópe thóu in the Lórd, and kéep his wáy ;
and hé shall promóte thee, that thóu shalt
posséss *the* lánd : whén the ungódly shall pérish,
thou shalt sée it.

36 I mysélf have séen the ungódly in gréat
pów-er : and flóurishing líke *a* gréen báy-tree.

37 I went bý, and ló, he *was* góne : I sóught
him, but his pláce could *nó*-where be foúnd.

38 Kéep ínnocency, and take héed unto the
thíng that *is* ríght : for thát shall bríng a mán
péace at the lást.

39 'As for the transgréssors, théy shall pérish
to-*gé*-ther : and the énd of the ungódly is, théy
shall be róoted *óut* at the lást.

40 But the salvátion of the ríghteous cómeth
of *the* Lórd : who is álso their stréngth in the
tíme of tróu-ble.

41 And the Lórd shall stánd bý them, and *sáve*
them : he shall delíver them from the ungódly ;
and shall sáve them, becáuse they *pút* their
trúst in^hím.

  Glóry be to the Fáther, and to *the* Són : and
to the Hó-ly^Ghóst.

  As it wás in the begínning, is nów, and éver
sháll be : wórld with-*óut* énd.   A-men.

THE 8th EVENING

PSALM 41   *Beatus qui intelligit*   TONE III

B LÉSSED is hé that consídereth the *póor*
and néed-y : the Lórd shall delíver him in
the *time* öf tróu-blè.

2 The Lórd presérve him, and kéep him alíve,
that hé may be *bléss*-ed^up-on éarth : and delíver
nót thou hím into the wíll *öf* hïs én-e^mıes.

3 The Lórd cómfort him, whén he líeth *sick*
up^ón his béd : máke thou áll his béd *in* hïs
síck-ness.

4 I saíd, Lórd, be *mér*-ci^ful^ún-to mé : héal
my sóul, for I have sín-*nëd* ä-gaínst thee.

5 Mine énemies spéak *é*-vil of me : Whén shall
he díe, and *hïs* näme pé-rısh ?

6 And íf he cóme to sée me, he *spéak*-eth^
vá-ni-ty : and his héart concéiveth fálsehood
withín himsélf ; and whén he cómeth *förth* hë
téll-eth^ıt.

7 'All mine énemies whísper to-*gé*-ther^a-gaínst
mé : éven agaínst mé do théy imá-*gıne* thïs
é-vıl.

8 Lét the séntence of guíltiness pro-*céed* a-gaínst
him : and nów that he líeth, lét *him* rïse úp
no^more.

9 Yéa, éven mine ówn famíliar fríend, *whom*
I trúst-ed : who did álso éat of my bréad, hath
laïd grëat wáit for^me.

10 But bé thou mérciful *un*-to^mé, O Lórd :
raíse thou me úp agaín, and I *shäll* rë-wárd
them.

11 By thís I knów thou *fá*-vour-est mé : that
mine énemy doth not trí-*ümph* ä-gaínst më.

12 And whén I am ín my héalth, *thou* up-^
-hóld-est me : and shalt sét me befóre thy *fäce*
för év-er.

13 Bléssed be the Lórd *Gód* of^Is-ra-el : wórld
with-*öut* ënd.   A-men.

Glóry be to the *Fá*-ther,^and^to the Són : and
tö thë Hó-ly^Ghòst.

As it wás in the begínning, is nów, and *év*-er
sh* áll be : wórld with-*öut* ënd.   A-men.

PSALM 42   *Quemadmodum*   TONE VII

LÍKE   AS   the   hárt   de-*sír*-eth^the   wá^ter-
     -bróoks : so lóngeth my sóul *af*-ter thée,
O^Gód.

2 My sóul is athírst for Gód, yéa, éven *for*
the lív^ing Gód : whén shall I cóme to appéar
befóre the *pré*-sence of Gód ?

3 My téars have béen my *méat* dáy and **níght :**

whíle they daíly sáy unto me, *Whére* is nów thy⌢Gód ?

4 Now whén I thínk thereupon, I póur out my *héart* by my-sélf : for I wént with the múlti-tude; and bróught them fórth ín-*to* the hóuse of⌢Gód ;

5 In the voíce of *praíse* and⌢thanks-gív-ing : amóng súch *as* keep hó-ly⌐dáy.

6 Whý art thóu so fúll of *héa*-vi⌐ness, O⌢my sóul : and whý art thou só disquíet-*ed* with-ín me ?

7 *Pút* thy trúst⌢in Gód : for I will yét give him thánks for the hélp *of* his cóun-te⌐nance.

8 My Gód, my sóul is *véx*-ed⌢with-ín me : thérefore will I remémber thee concérning the lánd of Jórdan ; and the líttle *híll* of Hér-mon.

9 'One deep cálleth anóther, becáuse of the *noíse* of⌢the wá⌐ter-pípes : áll thy wáves and stórms *are* gone ó-ver⌢mé.

10 The Lórd hath gránted his lóving-kíndness *in* the dáy-time : and in the níght-séason did I síng of hím ; and máde my práyer unto the *Gód* of my lífe.

11 I will sáy unto the Gód of my stréngth ; Whý hast *thóu* for-gót⌐ten mé : whý go I thús héavily ; whíle the éne-*my* op-prés-seth⌢me ?

12 My bónes are smítten a-*sún*-der⌢as wíth⌢a swórd : while mine énemies that tróuble me *cást* me in the⌢téeth ;

13 Námely, while they say *dái*-ly ún⌐to me : *Whére* is nów thy⌢Gód ?

14 Whý art thóu so *véx*-ed, O⌃my sóul : and whý art thou só disquíet-*ed* with-ín me ?

15 O *pút* thy trúst⌃in Gód : for I will yét thánk him, which is the hélp of my cóun-*te*-nance, and my⌃Gód.

Glóry be to the *Fá*-ther,⌃and to⌃the Són : and *to* the Hó-ly⌃Ghóst.

As it wás in the begínning, is nów, and *év*-er shall be : wórld with-*óut* énd.   A-men.

Psalm 43   *Judica me Deus*   Tone V

GIVE SÉN-tence with me, O Gód, and defénd my cáuse against the ungódly *péo*-ple : O delíver me from the de-*ceit*-ful and wíck⌃ed män.

2 For thóu art the Gód of my stréngth ; whý hast thou pút me *fróm* thee : and whý go I so héavily, while the éne-*my* op-préss⌃eth më ?

3 O sénd óut thy líght and thy trúth, that théy may *léad* me : and bríng me únto thy hóly híll, and *to* thy dwéll-īng.

4 And that 'I may gó únto the áltar of Gód ; éven únto the Gód of my jóy and *glád*-ness : and upón the hárp will I give thánks unto *thée*, O Gód,⌃my Göd.

5 Whý art thóu so héavy, O my *sóul* : and whý art thou só disquíet-*ed* with-ín më ?

6 O pút thy trúst in *Gód* : for I will yét give him thánks, which is the hélp of my *cóun-te*-nance, and⌃my Göd.

Glóry be to the Fáther, and to the *Són* : and *to* the Hó⌓ly Ghöst.

As it wás in the begínning, is nów, and ever *sháll* be : wórld with-*óut* énd.   A-mën.

THE 9th EVENING

PSALM 47   *Omnes gentes plaudite*   TONE V

O CLÁP your hánds togéther, áll ye *péo*-ple : O síng unto Gód with the *voíce* of mé-lo⌓dy.

2 For the Lórd is hígh, and to be *féar*-ed : he is the gréat *Kíng* up-on áll the⌃éarth.

3 Hé shall subdúe the péople únder *us* : and the nátions *ún*-der óur feet.

4 Hé shall chóose óut an héritage for *ús* : éven the wórship of Jácob, *whóm* he lóv-ed.

5 Gód is gone úp with a mérry *noíse* : and the Lórd with the *sóund* of the trúmp.

6 O síng praíses ; síng praíses únto our *Gód :* O síng praíses ; síng praíses *ún*-to our Kíng.

7 For Gód is the Kíng of áll the *éarth* : síng ye praíses with *ún*-der-stánd-ing.

8 Gód reígneth óver the *héa*-then : Gód sítteth up-*ón* his hó-ly⌢séat.

9 The prínces of the péople are joíned unto the péople of the Gód of *Á*-bra⌐ham : for Gód, which is véry hígh exálted ; doth defénd the eárth, as it *wére* with a shíeld.

Glóry be to the Fáther, and to the *Són* : and *to* the Hó-ly⌢Ghóst.

As it wás in the begínning, is nów, and ever *sháll* be : wórld with-*óut* énd.   A-men.

Psalm 48   *Magnus Dominus*   Tone VII

REAT IS the Lórd, and híghly *to* be praís-ed : in the cíty of our Gód, éven up-*ón* his hó⌐ly híll.

2 The híll of Sýon is a faír pláce, and the *jóy* of⌢the whóle eárth : upón the nórth-síde líeth the cíty of the gréat Kíng ; Gód is well knówn in her pálaces *as* a⌢súre ré-füge.

3 For ló, the *kíngs* of the eárth : are gáthered, and góne *by* to-gé-thër.

4 They márvell-*ed* to sée⌢such thíngs : they were astónished, and *súd*-den⌐ly cást döwn.

5 Féar came thére upón *them*, and sór-row : ás upón a wóman *in* her trá-vaïl.

6 Thóu shalt bréak the *shíps* of the séa : *thróugh* the eást-wïnd.

7 Líke as we have héard, só have we séen in the cíty of the Lórd of hósts ; in the cí-ty^of óur Gód : Gód uphóldeth the *sáme* for év-ër.

8 We waít for thy lóving-*kínd*-ness, O Gód : in the *mídst* of^thy tém-plë.

9 O Gód, accórding to thy Náme, só is thy praíse *ún*-to^the wórld's énd : thy ríght hánd is *fúll* of rígh^teous-nëss.

10 Lét the móunt Sýon rejoíce, and the dáughter of *Jú*-dah be glád : becáuse *of* thy júdge-mënts.

11 Wálk about Sýon, and go *róund* a-bóut her : and téll the *tów*-ers there-öf.

12 Márk well her búlwarks, sét *up* her hóus-es : that yé may téll them *that* come áf-tër.

13 For thís Gód is óur Gód for *év*-er^and év-er : hé shall bé our *guíde* un-to dëath.

Glóry be to the *Fá*-ther,^and to^the Són : and *to* the Hó^ly Ghöst.

As it wás in the begínning, is nów, and *év*-er sh. II be : wórld with-*óut* énd.   A-mën.

PSALM 40   *Audite hæc omnes*   TONE IV

O HÉAR ye thís, *áll* ye péo-ple : pónder it with your éars, all *yé* that dwéll ïn the^ wórld ;

2 Hígh and lów, *rích* and póor : *óne* with an-öth-er.

3 My móuth shall *spéak* of wís-dom : and my
héart shall múse *of* ún-der-ständ-ing.

4 I will inclíne mine éar *to* the pá-ra⌒ble : and
shéw my *dárk* spéech up-ön the⌒hárp.

5 Whérefore should I féar in the *dáys* of
wíck-ed⌒ness : and whén the wíckedness of my
héels cóm-*pass*-eth me röund a⌒bóut ?

6 There be sóme that pút their trúst *in* their
góods : and bóast themsélves in the múlti-*tude*
of their rĭch-es.

7 But nó mán may delí-*ver* his bró-ther : nor
máke agrée-*ment* un-to Göd for⌒him ;

8 For it cóst móre to re-*déem* their sóuls : só
that hé must lét that *a*-lóne for ëv-er ;

9 Yéa, though *he* líve lóng : — and sée nöt the⌒
gráve.

10 For he séeth that wíse men álso díe, and
pé-*rish* to-gé-ther : as wéll as the ígnorant and
fóolish, and léave their *rich*-es for öth-er.

11 And yét they thínk that their hóuses shall
contín-*ue* for év-er : and that their dwélling-
pláces shall endúre from óne generátion to
anóther ; and cáll the lánds *áf*-ter their öwn námes.

12 Névertheless, mán will nót a-*bíde* in hó-nour :
séeing he may be compáred unto the béasts that
pérish ; *this* is the wäy of⌒thém.

13 Thís *is* their fóol-ish⌒ness : and their postéri-*ty*
praíse their säy-ing.

14 They líe in the héll like shéep ; déath gnáweth
upón them, and the ríghteous shall háve dominá-

tion óver them *in* the mórn-ing : their béauty shall
consúme in the sépulchre *óut* of their dwéll-ing.

15 But Gód hath delívered my sóul from the
pláce of héll : for *hé* shall re-ceïve me.

16 Bé not thóu afraíd, though óne *be* máde rích :
or if the glóry of his *hóuse* be ín-crëas-ed ;

17 For hé shall cárry nóthing awáy with him
whén he dí-eth : neíther *shall* his pómp föl-low⌢
him.

18 For whíle he líved, he cóunted himself an
*háp-*py mán : and so lóng as thou dóest wéll unto
thysélf, *mén* will spéak göod of⌢thee.

19 Hé shall fóllow the génerátion *of* his fá-thers:
and *shall* né-ver sëe líght.

20 Mán béing in hónour hath nó *un-*der-stánd-
-ing : but is compáred unto *the* béasts that pë-rish.

    Glóry be to the Fáther, and *to* the Són : *and*
to the Hö-ly⌢Ghóst.

    As it wás in the begínning, is nów, and *év-*er
sháll be : wórld *with-*óut énd.   À-men.

THE 10th EVENING

PSALM 53   *Dixit insipiens*   TONE I

T HE FÓOL-ish bódy hath saíd in *his* héart :
   Thére is nö Göd.

2 Corrúpt are théy, and becóme abóminable

in their wíck-*ed*-ness : there is *nóne* that dö-eth⌒
göod.

3 Gód looked dówn from héaven upon the
chíldren *of* mén : to sée if there were ány that
would understánd, *and* séek äf-ter⌒Göd.

4 But théy are áll gone óut of the wáy ; théy
are altogéther becóme abómi-*na*-ble : there is
álso nóne that dó-*eth* góod, nö not⌒öne.

5 Aré not théy withóut understánding that
wórk wíck-*ed*-ness : éating up my péople as íf
they would éat bréad ? they háve not cáll-*ed*
up-ön Göd.

6 Théy were afraíd where nó *fear* wás : for
Gód hath bróken the bónes of hím that besíeged
thee ; thou hast pút them to confúsion, becáuse
Gód ·*hath* des-pīs-ed⌒thëm.

7 'Oh, that the salvátion were gíven unto
'Israel out of *Sý*-on : 'Oh, that the Lórd would
delíver his péople óut *of* cap-tī-vi⌐tÿ !

8 Thén should Jácob *re*-joíce : and 'Israel
should bè rīght gläd.

Glóry be to the Fáther, and to *the* Són : and
to the Hö-ly⌒Ghöst.

As it wás in the begínning, is nów, and éver
shall be : wórld with-*out* énd.   Ä-mën.

PSALM 54   *Deus in nomine*

1 Sáve me, O Gód, for thy *Náme's* sáke : and
avénge *me* in thÿ strëngth.

2 Héar my práyer, *O* Gód : and héarken unto the *wórds* of mÿ möuth.

3 For strángers are rísen up a-*gaínst* me : and týrants, which háve not Gód befóre their éyes, seek *áf*-ter mÿ söul.

4 Behóld, Gód is my *hélp*-er : the Lórd is with thém *that* up-höld my⌒söul.

5 He shall rewárd évil unto mine én-*e*-mies : destróy thou *thém* in thÿ trüth.

6 An óffering of a frée héart will I gíve thee, and praíse thy Náme, O Lórd : becaúse it is so *cóm*-fort-ä-blë.

7 For hé hath delívered me óut of áll my *tróu*-ble : and mine éye hath séen his desíre up-*ón* mine ën-eᵓmïes.

Glóry be to the Fáther, and to *the* Són : and *to* the Hö-ly⌒Ghöst.

As it wás in the begínning, is nów, and éver *sháll* be : wórld with-*óut* énd.   Ä-mën.

PSALM 55   *Exaudi Deus*   TONE II

HÉAR MY práyer, O *Gód* : and híde not thysélf from *mÿ* pë-ti-tion.

2 Take héed unto mé, and *héar* me : how I móurn in my práyer, *änd* ám véx-ed.

3 The énemy críeth só, and the ungodly cometh

ón so *fást* : for théy are mínded to dó me some
míschief ; so malíciously are they *sët* ä-gaínst me.

4 My héart is disquíeted with-*ĭn* me : and the
féar of déath is fáll-*ĕn* üp-ón me.

5 Féarfulness and trémbling are cóme up-*ón*
me : and an hórrible dréad hath *ö*-vër-whélm-ed
me.

6 And I saíd ; 'O that I had wíngs like a *dóve* :
for thén would I flée a-*wäy*, änd bé^at rést.

7 Ló, thén would I gét me awáy far *óff* : and
remaín *ĭn* thë wíl-der-ness.

8 I would máke háste to es-*cápe* : becáuse of
the stórmy *wĭnd* änd tém-pest.

9 Destróy their tóngues, O Lórd, and di-*víde*
them : for I have spíed unríghteousness and strífe
ĭn thë cí-ty.

10 Dáy and níght they gó abóut withín the wálls
there-*óf* : míschief álso and sórrow are *ĭn* thë
mídst^of it.

11 Wíckedness is there-*ĭn* : deceít and guíle go
not *öut* öf their stréets.

12 For it is nót an ópen énemy that hath dóne
me this dis-*hó*-nour : for thén I *cöuld* häve
bórne it.

13 Neíther was it mine advérsary, that did
mágnify himself a-*gaínst* me : for thén perad-
vénture I wóuld have híd *mÿ*-sëlf from him.

14 But it was éven thóu, my com-*pán*-ion : my
guíde, and mine *öwn* fä-mil-iar friend.

15 We tóok sweet cóunsel to-*gé*-ther : and wálked
in the *höuse* öf Gód^as fríends.

16 Let déath come hástily upón them ; and lét them gó down quíck into *héll* : for wíckedness is in their dwéllings, *änd* ä-móng them.

17 'As for mé, I will cáll upon *Gód* : and the *Lörd* shäll sáve me.

18 In the évening, and mórning, and at nóon-day will I práy ; and that *ín*-stant⁼ly : and *hë* shäll héar⌃my voíce.

19 It is hé that hath delívered my sóul in péace from the báttle that was a-*gáinst* me : for thére were *mä*-nÿ wíth me.

20 Yéa, even Gód, that endúreth for éver, shall héar me, and bríng them *dówn* : for they wíll not *türn*, nör féar Gód.

21 He laíd his hánds upon súch as be at péace with *him* : and he *bräke* hïs có⁼ve-nant.

22 The wórds of his móuth were sófter than bútter, having wár in his *héart* : his wórds were smóother than oíl, and yét *bë* thëy vé⁼ry swórds.

23 O cást thy búrden upon the Lórd, and hé shall *nóu*-rish⌃thee : and sháll not súffer the ríghteous to *fäll* för év-er.

24 And ás for *thém* : thóu, O Gód, shalt bríng them into the pít *öf* dë-strúc-tion.

25 The blóod-thírsty and deceítful mén shall not líve out hálf their *dáys* : nevertheless, my trúst shall *bë* ïn thée,⌃O Lórd.

Glóry be to the Fáther, and to the *Són* : and *tö* thë Hó⁼ly Ghóst.

As it wás in the begínning, is nów, and éver *sháll* be : wórld with-*öut* ënd.   A-men.

THE 11th EVENING

PSALM 59   *Eripe me de inimicis*   TONE III

DᴇʟÍv-er me from mine *én*-e⌒mies, O Gód :
defénd me from thém that ríse úp *a*-gaínst me.

2 O delíver me from the *wick*-ed dó-ers : and sáve me from the *blóod*-thírs-ty⌒mén.

3 For ló, they líe *wait*-ing⌒for my sóul : the míghty mén are gáthered against me; without any offénce or fáult *of* me, O⌒Lórd.

4 They rún and prepáre them-*selves* with⌒óut my fáult : aríse thou thérefore to hélp *me*, and be⌒hóld.

5 Stánd úp, O Lórd Gód of hósts, thou Gód of 'Israel ; to vísit *all* the héa-then : and bé not mérciful unto thém that offénd of mali-*cious* wíck-ed⌒ness.

6 They gó tó and *fró* in⌒the éve-ning : they grín like a dóg, and rún about thróugh *the* cí-ty.

7 Behóld, they spéak with their móuth, and *swórds* are⌒in their líps : *for* whó doth⌒héar ?

8 But thóu, O Lórd, shalt háve them *in* de-rí--sion : and thóu shalt láugh all the héa-*then* to scórn.

9 My stréngth will I as-*cribe* un-to thée : for thóu art the Gód of *my* ré-fuge.

10 Gód shéweth me his *góod*-ness^plén-teous-ly :
and Gód shall lét me sée my desíre upon *mine*
én-e^mies.

11 Sláy them nót, lest my *péo*-ple^for-gét it :
but scátter them abróad amóng the peóple ; and
pút them dówn, O Lórd, *our* de-fénce.

12 For the sín of their móuth, and for the wórds
of their líps, they shall be *tá*-ken^in their príde :
and whý ? their préaching is of cúrs-*ing* and líes.

13 Consúme them in thy wráth ; consúme them,
that *théy* may pé-rish : and knów that it is Gód
that rúleth in Jácob ; and únto the énds *of* the
wórld.

14 And in the évening *théy* will re-túrn : grín like
a dóg, and will gó abóut *the* cí-ty.

15 Théy will rún *hére* and^thére for méat : and
grúdge if they be not sá-*tis*-fi-ed.

16 'As for mé, I will síng of thy pówer ; and will
praíse thy mércy betímes *in* the mórn-ing : for
thóu hast béen my defénce and réfuge in the dáy
of *my* tróu-ble.

17 Unto thée, O my *stréngth*, will I síng : for
thóu, O Gód, art my réfuge, and my mér-*ci*-ful
Gód.

Glóry be to the *Fá*-ther,^and^to the Són : and
to *the* Hó-ly^Ghóst.

As it wás in the begínning, is nów, and *év*-er
sháll be : wórld withóut *énd*. A-men.

PSALM 60   *Deus repulisti nos*   TONE VIII

O GÓD, thou hast cást us óut, and scáttered
us a-*bróad* : thou hast álso béen displéased ;
O túrn thee *ún*-to ús a⌢gaīn.

2 Thóu hast móved the lánd, and di-*vĭ*-ded⌢it :
héal the sóres theréof, *for* it shá-këth.

3 Thóu hast shéwed thy péople héavy *things* :
thou hast gíven us a *drĭnk* of déad-ly⌢wīne.

4 Thóu hast gíven a tóken for súch as *féar* thee :
that théy may tríumph be-*cáuse* of the trüth.

5 Thérefore were thý belóved de-*lĭ*-ver⌢ed :
hélp me with thy ríght *hánd*, and héar më.

6 Gód hath spóken in his hóliness ; I will
rejoíce, and divíde *Sý*-chem : and méte óut the
vál-*ley* of Súc-cöth.

7 Gílead is míne, and Manásses is *mĭne* :
'Ephraim álso is the stréngth of my héad ; Júdah
is my láw-gív⌢ër ;

8 Móab is my wásh-pot ; over 'Edom will I
cást óut my *shóe* : Phĭlístia, *bé* thou glád of⌢më.

9 Whó will léad me ínto the strong *cĭ*-ty : whó
will bríng me *ĭn*-to 'E-döm ?

10 Hást not thou cást us óut, O *Gód* : wĭlt not
thóu, O Gód, go *óut* with óur hösts ?

11 O be thóu our hélp in *tróu*-ble : for vaín *is* the
hélp of⌢män.

12 Through Gód will we dó great *ácts* : for
it is hé that shall tréad *dówn* our én-e⸗mïes.

Glóry be to the Fáther, and to the *Són* : and
to the Hó-ly⁀Ghöst.

As it wás in the begínning, is nów, and éver
sháll be : wórld with-*óut* énd.   A-mën.

PSALM 61   *Exaudi Deus*   TONE IV

H ÉAR MY crý-*ing*, O Gód : give éar únto
   my práyer.

2 From the énds of the éarth will I cáll *up*-on
thée : whén my héart is in héa-*vi*-ness.

3 O sét me úp upon the róck that is hígh-*er*
than 'I : for thóu hast béen my hópe ; and a stróng
tówer for me agaínst the én-*e*-my.

4 I will dwéll in thy táberna-*cle* for év-er : and
my trúst shall be únder the cóvering of *thý*
wíngs.

5 For thóu, O Lórd, hast héard *my* de-síres :
and hast gíven an héritage unto thóse that féar
thy Náme.

6 Thóu shalt gránt the Kíng *a* lóng lífe : that
his yéars may endúre throughóut all géne-*rá*-
tions.

7 Hé shall dwéll before *Gód* for év-er : O prepáre
thy lóving mércy and faíthfulness ; that théy
may pre-*sérve* him.

8 Só will I álway sing praíse ún-*to* thy Náme : that I may daíly perfórm *my* vóws.

Glóry be to the Fáther, and *to* the Són : and to the Hó-*ly* Ghóst.

As it wás in the begínning, is nów, and *év*-er sháll be : wórld withóut énd.   *A*-men.

THE 12th EVENING

PSALM 65   *Te decet hymnus*   TONE VII

THÓU, O Gód, art *prais*-ed⌐in Sý-on : and unto thée shall the vów be perfórmed *in* Je-rú⸗sa-lëm.

2 Thóu that *héar*-est the práyer : unto *thée* shall áll⌐flesh cöme.

3 My misdéeds pre-*vaíl* a-gaínst me : O bé thou mérciful *ún*-to our síns.

4 Bléssed is the mán, whom thou chóosest, and re-*ceív*-est ún⸗to thée : hé shall dwéll in thy córt ; and shall be sátisfied with the pléasures of thy hóuse, éven of thy *hó*-ly tém-plë.

5 Thóu shalt shéw us wónderful thíngs in thy ríghteousness, O Gód of *our* sal-vá-tion : thóu that árt the hópe of áll the énds of the éarth ; and of thém that remaín *in* the bróad sëa.

6 Whó in his stréngth sétteth *fást* the móun-
-tains : and is gírded a-*bóut* with pów-ër.

7 Who stílleth the *rá*-ging of⌢the séa : and the
noíse of his wáves, and the mádness *of* the péo-plë.

8 Théy álso that dwéll in the úttermost párts
of the eárth shall be a-*fráid* at⌢thy tó-kens : thóu
that mákest the óutgoings of the mórning and
éve-ning⌢to praíse thëe.

9 Thou vísitest the *eárth*, and bléss⌒est it : thou
mákest it *vé*-ry plén-t ëous.

10 The ríver of Gód is *fúll* of wá-ter : thou
prepárest their córn ; for só thou pro-*ví*-dest for⌢
the ëarth.

11 Thou wáterest her fúrrows ; thou séndest
raín into the líttle *vál*-leys there-óf : thou mákest
it sóft with the dróps of raín, and bléssest the
in-crease of ït.

12 Thou crównest the yéar *with* thy góod-ness :
and thy *clóuds* drop fát-nëss.

13 They shall dróp upon the dwéllings *of* the
wíl⌒der-ness : and the líttle hílls shall re-*joíce* on
év⌒ery sïde.

14 The fólds *shall* be fúll⌢of shéep : the válleys
álso shall stánd so thíck with córn, that *they* shall
láugh⌢and sïng.

Glóry be to the *Fá*-ther,⌢and to⌢the Són : and
to the Hó⌒ly Ghöst.

As it wás in the begínning, is nów, and *év*-er
sháll be : wórld with-*óut* énd.   A-mën.

PSALM 66   *Jubilate Deo*   TONE **V**

O BE jóyful in Gód, áll ye *lánds* : síng práises unto the hónour of his Náme ; máke his praíse *to* be gló-ri-ous.

2 Sáy unto Gód, O how wónderful art thóu in thy *wórks* : thróugh the gréatness of thy pówer shall thine énemies be fóund *li*-ars un-to^thée.

3 For áll the wórld shall wórship *thée* : síng of *thée*, and praíse thy^Náme.

4 O cóme híther, and behóld the wórks of *Gód* : how wónderful he ís in his dóing towárd the *chíl*-dren of mén.

5 He túrned the séa into drý *lánd* : só that they wént through the wáter on fóot ; thére did *wé* re-joíce there-of.

6 He rúleth with his pówer for éver ; his éyes behóld the *péo*-ple : and súch as wíll not belíeve shall nót be áble *to* ex-ált them-selves.

7 O praíse our Gód, ye *péo*-ple : and máke the voíce of his *praíse* to be héard ;

8 Who hóldeth our sóul in *life* : and súffereth *nót* our féet to^slíp.

9 For thóu, O Gód, hast *pró*-ved^us : thou álso hast tríed us, líke as síl-*ver* is trí-ed.

10 Thou bróughtest us ínto the *snáre* : and laídest tróu-*ble* up-ón our^lóins.

11 Thou súfferedst mén to ríde óver our *héads* :
we wént through fíre and wáter ; and thou
bróughtest us óut ín-*to* a wéal-thy^pláce.

12 I will gó into thine hóuse with búrnt-*óf*-fer͞
-ings : and will páy thee my vóws ; which I prómised with my líps, and spáke with my móuth,
when I *was* in tróu-ble.

13 I will óffer unto thée fát burnt-sácrifices, with
the íncense of *ráms* : I will óffer *búl*-locks and
góats.

14 O cóme híther, and héarken, all yé that féar
Gód : and I will téll you what hé hath *dóne* for
mý sóul.

15 I cálled unto hím with my *móuth* : and gáve
him *práis*-es with my^tóngue.

16 If I inclíne unto wíckedness with mine *héart* :
the Lórd *will* not héar me.

17 But Gód hath *héard* me : and consídered the
vóice of my práyer.

18 Praísed be Gód who hath nót cast óut my
práyer : nor túrned his *mér*-cy fróm me.

Glóry be to the Fáther, and to the *Són* : and
to the Hó-ly^Ghóst.

As it wás in the begínning, is nów, and éver
sháll be : wórld with-*óut* énd.   A-men.

PSALM 67   *Deus misereatur*   TONE VI

GOD BE mérciful unto *ús*, and bléss us : and
shéw us the líght of his cóuntenance, and
be mér-*ci*-fül un-to ˆus ;

2 That thy wáy may be *knówn* up-on eárth : thy
sáving héalth a-*móng* äll ná-tions.

3 Lét the péople *praíse* thee, O Gód : yéa, let
áll the *péo*-plë praíse thée.

4 O lét the nátions-re-*joíce* and be glád : for
thóu shalt júdge the fólk ríghteously ; and góvern
the ná-*tions* üp-on eárth.

5 Lét the péople *praíse* thee, O Gód : let áll
the *péo*-plë praíse thée.

6 Thén shall the eárth bring *fórth* her ín-crease :
and Gód, éven our ówn Gód, shall gíve *us* hïs
bléss-ing.

7 *Gód* shall bléss ús : and áll the énds of the
wórld shäll féar hím.

Glóry be to the *Fá*-ther,ˆand toˆthe Són : and
to thë Hó-lyˆGhóst.

As it wás in the begínning, is nów, and *év*-er
sháll be : wórld with-*óut* ënd.   A-men.

THE 13th EVENING

PSALM 69   *Salvum me fac*   TONE I

SÁVE ME, O God : for the wáters are cóme
ín, éven *ún*-to my söul.

2 I stíck fást in the déep míre, where no
gróund is : I am cóme into déep wáters, so that
the *flóods* run ó꞉ver më.

3 I am wéary of crýing ; my thróat *is* drý :
my síght faíleth me for waíting so *lóng* up-on^my
Göd.

4 Théy that háte me withóut a cáuse are móre
than the haírs of *my* héad : théy that áre mine
énemies, and would destróy me guílt-*less*, are
mígh-tÿ.

5 I paíd them the thíngs that I né-*ver* tóok :
Gód, thou knówest my símpleness, and my fáults
are not híd^from thëe.

6 Lét not thém that trúst in thée, O Lórd
Gód of hósts, be ashámed for *my* cáuse : lét not
thóse that séek thee be confóunded through
mé ; O Lórd *Gód* of 'Is꞉ra-ël.

7 And whý? for thy sáke have I súffered
re-próof : sháme hath cóv-*er*-ed my fäce.

8 I am becóme a stránger unto my *bré*-thren :
éven an álien unto my *mó*-ther's chíl-drën.

9 For the zéal of thine hóuse hath éven éat-*en*

me : and the rebúkes of thém that rebúked thee are fál-*len* up-ón më.

10 I wépt, and chástened mysélf with *fást*-ing : and thát was túrn-*ed* to mý^re-pröof.

11 I pút on sáckcloth *ál*-so : and they jést-*ed* up-ón më.

12 Théy that sít in the gáte spéak a-*gaínst* me : and the drúnkards make *sóngs* up-ón më.

13 But, Lórd, I máke my práyer un-*to* thée : in an ac-*cép*-ta-ble tīme.

14 Héar me, O Gód, in the múltitude of thy *mér*-cy : éven in the trúth of *thý* sal-vá-tīon.

15 Táke me óut of the míre, that I *sínk* not : O lét me be delívered from thém that háte me ; and óut of *the* déep wá-tërs.

16 Lét not the wáter-flóod drówn me ; neíther let the déep swállow *me* úp : and lét not the pít shut her *móuth* up-ón më.

17 Héar me, O Lórd, for thy lóving-kíndness is cómfort-*a*-ble : túrn thee únto me accórding to the múltitude *of* thy mér-cīes.

18 And híde not thy fáce from thy sérvant, for 'I am in *tróu*-ble : O háste *thee*, and héar më.

19 Dráw nígh unto my sóul, and *sáve* it : O delíver me, becáuse *of* mine én^e-mīes.

20 Thóu hast knówn my repróof, my sháme, and my dis-*hón*-our : mine ádversaries are *áll* in thy sīght.

21 Thy rebúke hath bróken my héart ; I am fúll of héa-*vi*-ness : I lóoked for sóme to have

píty on me, but thére was nó mán ; neíther
fóund I á-*ny* to cóm˦fo̧rt më.

22 They gáve me gáll *to* éat : and whén I was
thírsty they gáve me *vi*-ne-gar^to drĭnk.

23 Lét their táble be máde a snáre to táke
themselves *with*-ál : and lét the thíngs that shóuld
have béen for their wéalth be unto thém an
occá-*sion* of fál-lĭng.

24 Lét their éyes be blínded, that they *sée* not :
and éver *bów* thou dówn^their bäcks.

25 Póur out thine indignátion up-*ón* them : and
lét thy wráthful displéa-*sure* take hóld^of thëm.

26 Lét their hábitation *be* voíd : and nó man to
dwéll in their tënts.

27 For they pérsecute hím whom thóu hast
smĭt-ten : and they tálk hów they may véx thém
whom *thóu* hast wóun-dëd.

28 Lét them fáll from óne wíckedness to an-*ŏ-*
-ther : and nót come ín-*to* thy rígh t˦eous-nëss.

29 Lét them be wíped óut of the bóok of the
lĭv-ing : and nót be wrítten a-*móng* the rígh-tëous.

30 'As for mé, when I am póor and in héa-*vi*-
ness : thy hélp, O *Gód*, shall líft^me üp.

31 I will praíse the Náme of Gód with *a* sóng :
and mágnify it *with* thánks-gív-ĭng.

32 This álso shall pléase *the* Lórd : bétter than
a búllock *that* hath hórns^and höofs.

33 The húmble shall consíder thís, and *be* glád :
séek ye áfter Gód, *and* your sóul^shall lĭve.

34 For the Lórd héareth *the* póor : and despíseth
not his pri⌒son-ërs.

35 Let héaven and eárth *praise* him : the séa,
and áll that *móv*-eth there-ïn.

36 For Gód will sáve Sýon, and buíld the cíties
of *Jú*-dah : that mén may dwéll thére, and háve
it *in* pos-sés-sïon.

37 The pósterity álso of his sérvants shall inhé-*rit*
it : and théy that lóve his *Náme* shall dwéll⌒
there-ïn.

Glóry be to the Fáther, and to *the* Són : and
to the Hó⌒ly Ghöst.

As it wás in the begínning, is nów, and éver
sháll be : wórld with-*óut* énd.   A-mën.

PSALM 70   *Deus in adjutorium*   TONE III

HÁSTE THEE, O Gód, *to* de⌒lív-er me :
make háste *to* hélp me, O Lórd.
2 Lét them be ashámed and confóunded that
séek *áf*-ter my sóul : lét them be túrned báckward
and pút to confúsion *that* wísh me é-vil.

3 Lét them for theír rewárd, be *soon* bróught
to sháme : that crý ó-ver me, Thére, thére.

4 But lét all thóse that séek thee be *jóy*-ful⌒and⌒
glád in thée : and let áll súch as delíght in thý
salvátion say álway, *The* Lórd be praís-ed.

D

5 'As for mé, I am póor *and* in^mí-se-ry : háste *thee* ún-to me, O^Gód.

6 Thóu art my hélper, and *mý* re-déem-er : O Lórd, *make* nó long tár-ry^ing.

Glóry be to the *Fá*-ther,^and^to the Són : *and* to the Hó-ly^Ghóst.

As it wás in the begínning, is nów, and *év*-er sháll be : wórld *with*-óut énd.   A-men.

THE 14th EVENING

PSALM 73   *Quam bonus Israel*   TONE II

TRÚLY Gód is lóving unto '*Is*-ra⌐el : éven unto súch as áre of *a* cléan héart.

2 Névertheless, my féet were álmost *góne* : my tréadings *had* wéll⌐nigh slípt.

3 And whý?   I was gríeved at the *wtc*-ked : I do álso sée the ungódly in súch *pros*-pé⌐ri-ty.

4 For théy are in nó péril of *déath* : but are lús-*ty* and stróng.

5 They cóme in nó misfórtune like óther *fólk* : neíther are they plágued *like* óth⌐er mén.

6 And thís is the cáuse that théy are so hólden with *príde* : and óverwhélmed *with* crú⌐el-ty.

7 Their éyes swéll with *fát*-ness : and they do é-*ven* whát^they lúst.

8 They corrúpt óther, and spéak of wícked *blás*-phe͜my : their tálking is agaínst *the* móst Hígh.

9 For they strétch forth their móuth únto the *héa*-ven : and their tóngue gó-*eth* thróugh⌒the wórld.

10 Thérefore fáll the péople *ún*-to⌒them : and théreout súck they no smáll *ad*-ván-tage.

11 Túsh, say théy, hów should Gód per-*ceíve* it : is there knówledge in *the* móst Hígh ?

12 Ló, thése are the ungódly ; thése prósper in the wórld, and thése have ríches in pos-*sés*-sion : and I saíd ; Thén have I cléansed my héart in vaín, and wáshed mine hánds in ín-*no*-cen-cy.

13 'All the day lóng have I been *pún*-ish͜ed : and chástened éver-*y* mórn-ing.

14 Yéa, and I had álmost saíd éven as *théy* : but ló, thén I should have condémned the generátion of *thy* chíl-dren.

15 Thén thought 'I to understánd *thís* : but it wás *too* hárd⌒for mé,

16 Until I wént into the sánctuary of *Gód* : thén understóod I the énd *of* thése mén ;

17 Námely, hów thou dost sét them in slíppery *plá*-ces : and cástest them dówn, and *de*-stróy͜est thém.

18 'Oh, how súddenly do théy con-*súme* : pérish, and cóme to *a* féar͜ful énd !

19 Yéa, éven like as a dréam when one a-*wá*-keth :

só shalt thou máke their ímage to vánish óut of *the* cí-ty.

20 Thús my heárt was *gríev*-ed : and it went é-*ven* thróugh^my reíns.

21 So fóolish was I, and *íg*-no^rant : éven as it were a béast *be*-fóre thee.

22 Névertheless, I am álway *bý* thee : for thóu hast hólden me bý *my* ríght hánd.

23 Thóu shalt guíde me with thy *cóun*-sel : and after thát receíve me *with* gló-ry.

24 Whóm have I in héaven but *thée* : and there is nóne upon eárth that I desíre in compári-*son* of thée.

25 My flésh and my heárt *faíl*-eth : but Gód is the stréngth of my heárt ; and my pórtion *for* év-er.

26 For ló, they that forsáke thee shall *pé*-rish : thou hast destróyed all thém that commít fornicátion *a*-gaínst thée.

27 But it is góod for me to hóld me fást by Gód ; to pút my trúst in the Lórd *Gód* : and to spéak of áll thy wórks in the gátes of the dáughter *of* Sý-on.

    Glóry be to the Fáther, and to the *Són* : and to *the* Hó^ly Ghóst.

    As it wás in the begínning, is nów, and éver *sháll* be : wórld withóut *énd*.   A-men.

PSALM 74   *Ut quid Deus*   TONE IV

O GOD, whérefore art thou ábsent from *us* só lóng : whý is thy wráth so hót against the shéep of thy pás-*ture* ?

2 O thínk upón thy *cón*-gre-gá-tion : whom thóu hast púrchased, and redéemed of *óld*.

3 Thínk upon the tríbe of *thíne* in-hé-ri-tance : and móunt Sýon, wheréin thou hast *dwélt*.

4 Líft up thy féet, that thóu mayest útterly destróy *év*-ery én-e-my : which hath done évil in thy sánctua-*ry*.

5 Thine ádversaries róar in the mídst of thy *cón*-gre-gá-tions : and sét up their bánners for tó-*kens*.

6 Hé that héwed tímber afóre óut of *the* thíck trées : was knówn to bríng it to an éxcellent *wórk*.

7 But nów they bréak down áll the cárved *wórk* there-óf : with áxes and hám-*mers*.

8 They have sét fíre upon thy *hó*-ly plá-ces : and have defíled the dwélling-pláce of thy Náme, éven únto the *gróund*.

9 Yéa, they saíd in their héarts; Lét us make hávock of them *ál*-to-ge-ther : thús have they búrnt up áll the hóuses of Gód in the *lánd*.

10 We sée not our tókens; thére is nót óne

pró-phet móre : nó, not óne is there amóng us, that únderstándeth ány *móre*.

11 O Gód, how lóng shall the ádversary do *this* dis-hó-nour : how lóng shall the énemy blasphéme thy Náme, for év-*er* ?

12 Whý withdráwest *thóu* thy hánd : whý plúckest thou nót thy ríght hánd óut of thy bósom to consúme the éne-*my* ?

13 For Gód is my *Kíng* of óld : the hélp that is dóne upon éarth he dóeth it him-*sélf*.

14 Thóu didst divíde the séa *through* thy pów-er : thou brákest the héads of the drágons in the wá-*ters*.

15 Thou smótest the héads of Levía-*than* in píe-ces : and gávest him to be méat for the péople in the wílder-*ness*.

16 Thou bróughtest out fóuntains and wáters óut of *the* hárd rócks : thou dríedst up míghty wá-*ters*.

17 The dáy is thíne, and the *níght* is thíne : thóu hast prepáred the líght and the *sún*.

18 Thóu hast sét áll the bórders *of* the éarth : thóu hast máde súmmer and wín-*ter*.

19 Remémber thís, O Lórd, how the énemy *hath* re-bú-ked : and hów the fóolish péople hath blasphémed thy *Náme*.

20 O delíver nót the sóul of thy túrtle-dove únto the múltitude *of* the én-e⊃mies : and fórget nót the congregátion of the póor for év-*er*.

21 Lóok up-*ón* the có-ve⊃nant : for áll the éarth is fúll of dárkness, and crúel habitá-*tions*.

22 O lét not the símple gó a-*wáy* a-shám-ed : but lét the póor and néedy give praíse únto thy *Náme.*

23 Aríse, O Gód, maintaín *thine* ówn cáuse : remémber hów the fóolish mán blasphémeth thee dái-*ly.*

24 Forgét not the voíce *of* thine én-e^mies : the presúmption of thém that háte thee incréaseth ever móre and *móre.*

Glóry be to the Fáther, and *to* the Són : and to the Hóly *Ghóst.*

As it wás in the begínning, is nów, and *év*-er sháll be : wórld withóut énd.   A-*men.*

THE 15th EVENING

PSALM 78   *Attendite popule*   TONE I

HÉAR MY láw, O my *péo*-ple : inclíne your éars unto the *wórds* of mý móuth.

2 I will ópen my móuth in a pá-*ra*-ble : I will decláre hard *sén*-ten-ces of^óld ;

3 Which wé have héard *and* knówn : and súch as our fá-*thers* have tóld us ;

4 That we shóuld not híde them from the chíldren of the generátions *to* cóme : but to shéw the hónour of the Lórd ; his míghty and wónderful *wórks* that hé hath^dóne.

5 He máde a cóvenant with Jácob, and gave
Israel *a* láw : which he commánded our fore-
fáthers to *téach* their chíl-dren ;

6 That theír postérity might *knów* it : and the
chíldren *which* were yét un⸗bórn ;

7 To the intént that when théy *came* úp : théy
might shéw their *chíl*-dren the sáme ;

8 That théy might pút their trúst *in* Gód : and
nót to forgét the wórks of Gód ; but to kéep *his*
com-mánd-ments ;

9 And nót to bé as their forefáthers ; a faíthless
and stúbborn géne-*rá*-tion : a generátion that sét
not their héart aríght ; and whose spírit cléaveth
not stéd-*fast*-ly ún-to^Gód ;

10 Líke as the chíldren of É-*phra*-ym : who
beíng hárnessed, and cárrying bóws ; túrned
themselves báck in the *dáy* of bát-tle.

11 They képt not the cóvenant *of* Gód : and
wóuld not *wálk* in hís láw ;

12 But forgát what hé *had* dóne : and the
wónderful wórks that he had *shéw*-ed for thém.

13 Márvellous thíngs did hé in the síght of our
fórefáthers, in the lánd of 'E-gypt : éven in the
fiéld of Zó-an.

14 He divíded the séa, and lét them *go* thróugh :
he máde the wáters to *stánd* on an héap.

15 In the dáy-time álso he léd them with *a*
clóud : and áll the níght thróugh *with* a líght
of^fíre.

16 He cláve the hárd rócks in the wíl-*der*-ness :

and gáve them drínk thereóf, as it had been óut
of the gréat dépth.

17 He bróught wáters óut of the stó-*ny* róck : so
that it gúshed out *like* the rí-vers.

18 Yét for áll thís they sínned móre a-*gaínst* hím :
and provóked the most Híghest *in* the wíl-der-ness.

19 They témpted Gód in *their* héarts : and requíred *méat* for their lúst.

20 They spáke agaínst Gód also, *sáy*-ing : Shall
Gód prepáre a táble *in* the wíl-der-ness ?

21 He smóte the stóny róck indéed; that the
wáter gushed óut, and the stréams flówed
with-ál : but cán he give bréad álso ; or províde
flésh *for* his péo-ple ?

22 Whén the Lórd heard this, hé *was* wróth : so
the fíre was kíndled in Jácob; and there cáme
up héavy displéasure a-*gaínst* 'Is-ra-el ;

23 Becáuse they belíeved not *in* Gód : and pút
not their *trúst* in hís hélp.

24 Só he commánded the clóuds *a*-bóve : and
ópened the *dóors* of héa-ven.

25 He raíned dówn mánna álso upón them fór
to éat : and gáve them *fóod* from héa-ven.

26 So mán did eat án-*gels'* fóod : for he *sént* them
méat e-noúgh.

27 He cáused the eást-wínd to blów under
héa-ven : and thróugh his pówer he bróught in
the sóuth-wést-wínd.

28 He raíned flésh upón them as thíck *as* dúst :
and féathered fówls líke as the *sánd* of the séa.

29 He lét it fáll amóng *their* ténts : éven róund
abóut their *ha*-bi-tá-tion.

30 Só they did éat, and were wéll fílled ; for he
gáve them théir own *de*-síre : théy were nót
disappoínt-*ed* of theír lúst.

31 But whíle the méat was yét in their móuths ;
the héavy wráth of Gód came upón them, and
sléw the wéalthiest *of* thém : yéa, and smóte
dówn the chósen mén that *wére* in 'Is-ra⌐el.

32 But for áll thís they sínned *yet* móre : and
belíeved *not* his wón-drous⌐wórks.

33 Thérefore their dáys did hé consúme in
vá-*ni*-ty : and their *yéars* in tróu-ble.

34 Whén he sléw them, they *sóught* him : and
túrned them éarly, and en-*quír*-ed af-ter⌐Gód.

35 And they remémbered that Gód was *their*
stréngth : and that the hígh Gód was *theír*
re-déem-er.

36 Névertheless, they díd but flátter him with
their móuth : and dissémbled *with* him ín their⌐
tóngue.

37 For their héart was not whóle *with* hím :
neíther contínued they stédfast *in* his có-ve⌐nant.

38 But he was só mérciful, that he forgáve their
mís-deeds : and de-*stróy*-ed them nót.

39 Yéa, mány a tíme túrned he his wráth *a*-wáy :
and wóuld not súffer his whóle dis-*pléa*-sure to
a⌐ríse.

40 For he consídered that they wére *but* flésh :

and that they were éven a wínd that pásseth
awáy, and *cóm*-eth not a⌒gaín.

41 Mány a tíme did they provóke him in the
wíl-*der*-ness : and gríeved him *in* the dé-sert.

42 They túrned báck, and témp-*ted* Gód : and
móved the Hóly *One* in 'Is-ra⌒el.

43 They thoúght not of *his* hánd : and of the
dáy when he delívered them from the hánd *of*
the é-ne⌒my ;

44 Hów he had wróught his míracles in 'E-gypt :
and his wónders in the *field* of Zó-an.

45 He túrned their wáters in-*to* blóod : só that
they míght not drínk *of* the rí-vers.

46 He sént líce amóng them, and devóured *them*
úp : and frógs *to* de-stróy them.

47 He gáve their fruít unto the cáter-*pil*-lar :
and their lábour un-*to* the gráss-hop⌒per.

48 He destróyed their vínes with *hail*-stones :
and their múlberry-*trées* with the fróst.

49 He smóte their cáttle álso with *hail*-stones :
and their flócks *with* hót thún-der⌒bólts.

50 He cást upón them the fúriousness of his
wráth, ánger, displéasure, and *tróu*-ble : and sent
évil an-*gels* a-móng them.

51 He máde a wáy to his indignátion ; and spáred
not their sóul *from* déath : but gáve their lífe
óver *to* the pés-ti⌒lence ;

52 And smóte all the fírst-born in 'E-gypt : the
most príncipal and míghtiest in the *dwél*-lings of
Hám.

53 But ás for his ówn péople, he léd them fórth *like* shéep : and cárried them in the wíl-*der*-ness like a⌐flóck.

54 He bróught them óut sáfely, that they shóuld *not* féar : and óverwhélmed their é-*ne*-mies with the⌐séa.

55 And bróught them within the bórders of his sánctu-*a*-ry : éven to his móuntain which he púrchased *with* his ríght hánd.

56 He cást out the héathen álso be-*fóre* them : cáused their lánd to be divíded amóng them for **an** héritage ; and máde the tríbes of 'Israel to *dwéll* in their ténts.

57 Só they témpted, and displéased the móst *high* Gód : and képt not his *tés*-ti-mo-nies ;

58 But túrned their bácks, and féll awáy like their fóre-*fá*-thers : stárting asíde *like* a bró-ken⌐ bów.

59 For they gríeved him with their híll-*ál*-tars : and provóked him to displéasure *with* their í-ma⌐ges.

60 When Gód héard this, hé *was* wróth : and took sóre displéa-*sure* at 'Is-ra⌐el.

61 Só that he forsóok the tábernacle in *Sý*-lo : éven the tént that he had pítch-*ed* a-móng mén.

62 He delívered their pówer into captí-*vi*-ty : and their béauty into the *én*-e-my's hánd.

63 He gáve his péople óver álso únto *the* swórd : and was wróth with *his* in-hé-ri⌐tance.

64 The fíre consúmed their *yóung* mén : and their maídens were not gív-*en* to már-riage.

65 Their príests were slaín with *the* swórd : and there were nó wídows to make *lá*-men-tá-tion.

66 Só the Lórd awáked as óne out *of* sléep : and líke a gíant re-*frésh*-ed with wíne.

67 He smóte his énemies ín the hínd-*er* párts : and pút them to a per-*pé*-tu-al sháme.

68 He refúsed the tábernacle of *Jó*-seph : and chóse not the *tríbe* of 'E-phra͡ym ;

69 But chóse the tríbe of *Jú*-dah : éven the híll of Sýon *which* he lóv-ed.

70 And thére he buílt his témple *on* hígh : and laíd the foundátion of it líke the gróund which he hath *máde* con-tín-ual͡ly.

71 He chóse Dávid álso his *sér*-vant : and tóok him awáy *from* the shéep-folds.

72 As he was fóllowing the éwes gréat with yóung ones he *tóok* him : that he might féed Jácob his péople, and 'Israel *his* in-hé-ri͡tance.

73 Só he féd them with a faíthful and *trúe* heart : and rúled them prúdently with *áll* his pów-er.

Glóry be to the Fáther, and to *the* Són : and *to* the Hó-ly͡Ghóst.

As it wás in the begínning, is nów, and éver *shall* be : wórld with-*óut* énd.   A-men.

THE 16th EVENING

PSALM 82   *Deus stetit*   TONE VI

GOD STÁND-eth in the cóngre-*gá*-tion^of prin-ces : he is a *Judge* ä-mong gods.

2 How lóng will ye *give* wrong júdge-ment : and accépt the pérsons of *the* ün-gód-ly ?

3 Defénd the *póor* and fá^ther-less : see that súch as are in néed and necés-*si*-tÿ have ríght.

4 Delíver the *óut*-cast and póor : sáve them from the hánd of *the* ün-god-ly.

5 They will nót be léarned nor understánd ; but wálk on *still* in dárk-ness : áll the foundátions of the *earth* äre óut of ĉóurse.

6 I have *said*, Yé are góds : and yé are áll the chíldren of *the* möst Hígh-est.

7 But *yé* shall díe^like mén : and fáll like óne *of* thë prín-ces.

8 Aríse, O Gód, and *júdge* thou the éarth : for thóu shalt táke all héathen to *thine* ïn-hé-ri^tance.

Glóry be to the *Fá*-ther,^and to^the Són : and *to* thë Hó-ly^Ghóst.

As it wás in the begínning, is nów, and *év*-er sháll be : wórld with-*óut* ënd.   A-men.

PSALM 83   *Deus quis similis*   TONE IV

HOLD NOT thy tóngue, O Gód, keep *nót*
still sí-lence : refraín not thy-*sëlf*, O⌒Gód.

2 For ló, thine énemies *máke* a múr-mur⌐ing :
and théy that háte thee have líft up *thëir* héad.

3 Théy have imágined cráftily a-*gaïnst* thy
péo-ple : and táken cóunsel agaínst thy *së*-cret⌐
ónes.

4 Théy have saíd, Cóme, and lét us róot them
óut; that they bé no *móre* a péo-ple : and that
the náme of 'Israel may bé no móre in re-*mëm*-
brance.

5 For théy have cást their héads togéther with
óne con-sént : and are conféderate a-*gaïnst* thée ;

6 The tábernacles of the Édomites, *and* the
'Is-mael⌐ites : the Móabites, and *Hä*-gar⌐ens ;

7 Gébal, and 'Am-*mon*, and 'A-ma⌐lek : the
Phílistines, with thém that *dwëll* at⌒Týre.

8 'Assur álso is *joïn*-ed wíth them : and have
hólpen the chíldren *öf* Lót.

9 But dó thóu to thém as ún-*to* the Má-dian⌐ites :
unto Sísera, and unto Jábin at the bróok of
Kÿ-son ;

10 Who pérish-*ed* at Eñ-dor : and becáme as the
dúng *öf* the⌒éarth.

11 Make thém and their prínces like 'O-*reb* and

Zéb : yéa, make áll their prínces like as Zéba and
Säl-ma⊃na ;

12 Who sáy, Let us táke *to* our-sélves : the
hóuses of Gód in pos-*sĕs*-sion.

13 O my Gód, make them líke un-*to* a whéel :
and as the stúbble be-*före* the⌒wínd ;

14 Líke as the fíre that búrneth *up* the wóod :
and as the fláme that consúmeth the *möun*-tains.

15 Pérsecute them even só *with* thy tém-pest : and
máke them afraíd with *thÿ* stórm.

16 Máke their fáces a-shá-*med*, O Lórd : that théy
may *sĕek* thy⌒Náme.

17 Lét them be confŏunded and véxed éver
móre and móre : lét them be pút to sháme, and˙
pĕ-rish.

18 And théy shall knów that thóu, whose Náme
is Je-hó-vah : art ónly the móst Híghest óver *äll*
the⌒eárth.

Glóry be to the Fáther, and *to* the Són : and
to the *Hö*-ly⌒Ghóst.

As it wás in the begínning, is nów, and *év*-er
sháll be : wórld withóut énd.   *A*-men.

PSALM 84   *Quam dilecta*   TONE III

O HOW ámiable *are* thy dwéll-ings : *thou*
Lórd⌒of hösts !

2 My sóul hath a desíre and lónging to énter

into the *cóurts* of the Lórd : my héart and my flésh rejoíce in *the* lív‿ing Göd.

3 Yéa, the spárrow hath fóund her an hóuse; and the swállow a nést where *shé* may‿láy her yóung : éven thy áltars, O Lórd of hósts; my Kíng *and* my Göd.

4 Bléssed are théy that *dwéll* in thy hóuse : théy will be ál-*way* praís‿ing thëe.

5 Bléssed is the mán whose *stréngth* is in thée : in whose héart *are* thý wäys.

6 Who góing through the vále of mísery *úse* it‿fór a wéll : and the póols are fílled *with* wá-tër.

7 They will *gó* from‿stréngth to stréngth : and únto the Gód of góds appeareth évery one of thém *in* Sý-ön:

8 O Lórd Gód of *hósts*, héar my práyer : héarken, O Gód *of* Já-cöb.

9 Behóld, O *Gód* our‿de-fénd-er : and lóok upon the fáce of thíne *An*-oínt-ëd.

10 For one *dáy* in thy cóurts : is bétter than *a* thóu-sänd.

11 I had ráther be a dóor-keeper in the *hóuse* of my Gód : than to dwéll in the ténts of *un*-gód‿li-n ëss.

12 For the Lórd Gód is a *líght* and de-fénce : the Lórd will give gráce and wórship; and nó good thíng shall he withhóld from thém that líve *a* gód‿ly lïfe.

13 O *Lórd* Gód of hósts : bléssed is the mán that pútteth *his* trúst‿in thëe.

E

Glóry be to the *Fá*-ther,⌢and⌢to the Són : and to *the* Hó⌐ly Ghöst.

As it wás in the begínning, is nów, and *év*-er sháll be : wórld withóut *énd*. A-mën.

PSALM 85   *Benedixisti Domine*   TONE VIII

LÓRD, THOU art becóme grácious únto thy *lánd* : thóu hast túrned away the captívi-*ty* of Já⌐cob.

2 Thóu hast forgíven the offénce of thy *péo*-ple : and có-*ver*-ed áll⌢their⌢síns.

3 Thóu hast táken áway áll thy dis-*pléa*-sure : and túrned thysélf from thy wráthful *in*-dig-ná⌐tion.

4 Túrn us thén, O Gód our *Sá*-viour : and lét thine *án*-ger céase⌢from⌢us.

5 Wílt thou be displéased at ús for *év*-er : and wílt thou strétch out thy wráth from óne generá-tion *to* a-nó⌐ther ?

6 Wílt thou not túrn agaín, and *quíck*-en⌢us : that thy péople *may* re-joíce⌢in⌢thée ?

7 Shéw us thy mércy, O *Lórd* : and gránt us *thy* sal-vá⌐tion.

8 I will héarken what the Lórd Gód will sáy concérning *mé* : for hé shall speak péace unto his péople ; and to his saínts, that they túrn *nót* a-gaín.

9 For his salvátion is nígh thém that *féar* him :
that glóry may *dwéll* in óur^lánd.

10 Mércy and trúth are mét to-*gé*-ther : ríghteousness and péace have kís-*sed* each óth⌒er.

11 Trúth shall flóurish óut of the *éarth* : and
ríghteousness hath lóoked *dówn* from héa⌒ven.

12 Yéa, the Lórd shall shéw lóving-*kínd*-ness :
and our lánd shall *gíve* her ín⌒crease.

13 Ríghteousness shall gó be-*fóre* him : and hé
shall diréct his *gó*-ing ín^the^wáy.

Glóry be to the Fáther, and to the *Són* : and
to the Hó⌒ly^Ghóst.

As it wás in the begínning , is nów, and éver
shǎll be : wórld with-*óut* énd.   A⌒men.

THE 17th EVENING

Psalm 89   *Misericordias Domini*   Tone I

MY SÓNG shall be álway of the lóving-
kíndness of *the* Lórd : with my móuth
will I éver be shéwing thy trúth from óne
generátion *to* a-nó-ther.

2 For I have saíd ; Mércy shall be set úp for
év-er : thy trúth shalt thou stáblish *in* the
héa-vens.

3 I have máde a cóvenant with my *chó*-sen :
I have swórn unto Dá-*vid* my sér-vant ;

4 Thy séed will I stáblish for *év*-er : and sét up thy throne from óne generátion *to* a-nó-ther.

5 O Lórd, the véry héavens shall praíse thy wón-*drous* wórks : and thy trúth in the‿cón-gre-*gá*-tion of‿the saínts.

6 For whó is hé amóng *the* clóuds : that shall be compáred *un*-to the Lórd ?

7 And whát is hé amóng *the* góds : that shall be líke *un*-to the Lórd ?

8 Gód is véry gréatly to be féared in the cóuncil of *the* saínts : and to be hád in réverence of áll thém that are *róund* a-bóut him.

9 O Lórd Gód of hósts, whó is líke un-*to* thée : thy trúth, most míghty Lórd, *is* on év⸗ery síde.

10 Thou rúlest the ráging of *the* séa : thou stíllest the wáves there-*óf* when théy‿a-ríse.

11 Thou hast súbdued 'Egypt, and destróy-*ed* it : thou hast scáttered thine énemies abróad *with* thy mígh⸗ty árm.

12 The héavens are thíne; the éarth álso *is* thíne : thou hast laíd the foundátion of the róund wórld, and *áll* that thére⸗in is.

13 Thou hast máde the nórth and *the* sóuth : Tábor and Hérmon shall re-*joíce* in thý Náme.

14 Thou hást a mígh-*ty* árm : stróng is thy hánd, and hígh *is* thy ríght hánd.

15 Ríghteousness and équity are the habitátion of *thý* séat : mércy and trúth shall *gó* be-fóre‿thy fáce.

16 Bléssed is the péople, O Lórd, that can

rejoíce *in* thée : they shall wálk in the líght *of* thy cóun⌣te-nance.

17 Their delíght shall be daíly in *thy* Náme : and in thy ríghteousness *shall* they máke⌣their bóast.

18 For thóu art the glóry of *their* stréngth : and in thy lóving-kíndness thou shalt *líft* up our hórns.

19 For the Lórd is óur *de*-fénce : the Hóly One of 'Isra-*el* is óur Kíng.

20 Thou spákest sómetime in vísions unto thy saínts, *and* saídst : I have laíd hélp upon óne that is míghty ; I have exálted one chósen óut *of* the péo-ple.

21 I have fóund Dávid my *sér*-vant : with my hóly oíl have *I* an-oínt⌣ed him.

22 My hánd shall hóld *him* fást : and my *árm* shall stréngth⌣en him.

23 The énemy shall nót be áble to dó him ví-*o*-lence : the són of wíckedness *shall* not húrt him.

24 I will smíte dówn his fóes befóre *his* fáce : and plágue *them* that háte him.

25 My trúth álso and my mércy shall be *wíth* him : and in my Náme shall his hórn *be* ex-ált-ed.

26 I will sét his domínion álso in *the* séa : and his *ríght* hánd in⌣the flóods.

27 He shall cáll me ; Thóu art my *Fá*-ther : my Gód, and my *stróng* sal-vá-tion.

28 And I will máke him my *first*-born : hígher than the *kings* of the éarth.

29 My mércy will I kéep for hím for év-*er*-móre : and my cóvenant shall *stánd* fást with him.

30 His séed also will I máke to endure for *év*-er : and his thróne as the *dáys* of héa-ven.

31 But if his chíldren forsáke *my* láw : and wálk not *in* my júdge-ments ;

32 If they bréak my státutes, and kéep not mý com-*mánd*-ments : I will vísit their offénces with the ród ; and their *sín* with scóur-ges.

33 Névertheless, my lóving-kíndness will I not útterly táke *from* hím : nor súf-*fer* my trúth^to faíl.

34 My cóvenant will I not bréak ; nor álter the thíng that is gone óut of *my* líps : I have swórn ónce by my hóliness, that I will *nót* fail Dá-vid.

35 His séed shall endúre for *év*-er : and his séat is líke as the *sún* be-fóre me.

36 He shall stánd fást for évermore as *the* móon : and as the faíthful wít-*ness* in héa-ven.

37 But thóu hast abhórred and forsáken thine An-*oínt*-ed : and art dis-*pléas*-ed at him.

38 Thóu hast bróken the cóvenant of thy *sér*-vant : and cást his *crówn* to the gróund.

39 Thóu hast óverthrown áll his *hédg*-es : and bróken *dówn* his stróng hólds.

40 All théy that go bý *spoíl* him : and he is becóme a repróach *to* his neígh-bours.

41 Thóu hast sét up the ríght hánd of his é-*ne*-mies : and made áll his ádver-*sa*-ries to⌃ re-joíce.

42 Thóu hast táken awáy the édge of *his* swórd : and gívest him not víctory *in* the bát-tle.

43 Thóu hast put óut his *gló*-ry : and cást his thróne *dówn* to the gróund.

44 The dáys of his yóuth hast thou shórt-*en*-ed : and cóvered him *with* dis-hó-nour.

45 Lórd, how lóng wilt thou híde thysélf, for *év*-er : and sháll *thy* wráth búrn⌃like fíre ?

46 O remémber how shórt my *tíme* is : whérefore hast thou *máde* all mén⌃for nóught ?

47 What mán is he that líveth, and shall nót *see* déath : and sháll he delíver his sóul *from* the hánd⌃of héll ?

48 Lórd, whére are thy óld lóving-kínd-*ness*-es : which thou swárest unto Dá-*vid* in thý trúth ?

49 Remémber, Lórd, the rebúke that thy sér-*vants* have : and hów I do béar in my bósom the rebúkes of *má*-ny péo-ple ;

50 Whérewith thine énemies have blasphémed thee ; and slándered the fóotsteps of thíne An-*oínt*-ed : Praísed be the Lórd for évermore. A-*men*, and A-men.

   Glóry be to the Fáther, and to *the* Són : and *to* the Hó⌃ly Ghóst.

   As it wás in the begínning, is nów, and éver *sháll* be : wórld with-*óut* énd.   A-men.

THE 18th EVENING

PSALM 93   *Dominus regnavit*   TONE VIII

THE LÓRD is Kíng, and hath pút on
glórious ap-*pá*-rel : the Lórd hath pút on
his appárel, and gírd-*ed* him-sélf with⌢stréngth.

2 He hath máde the róund wórld so *súre* : that
it cán-*not* be móv-ed.

3 'Ever since the wórld begán hath thy séat
been pre-*pár*-ed : thóu art from *év*-er-last-ing.

4 The flóods are rísen, O Lórd ; the flóods have
lift úp their *voice* : the *flóods* lift úp their⌢wáves.

5 The wáves of the séa are míghty, and ráge
hór-ri⌢bly : but yét the Lórd, who dwélleth on
high, is mígh-ti⌢er.

6 Thy téstimonies, O Lórd, are véry *súre* :
hóliness becómeth thine *hóuse* for év-er.

Glóry be to the Fáther, and to the *Són* : and
to the Hó-ly⌢Ghóst.

As it wás in the begínning, is nów, and éver
sháll be : wórld with-*óut* énd.   A-men.

PSALM 94   *Deus ultionum*   TONE VII

O LÓRD Gód, · to whom *vén*-geance^be-
lóng-eth : thou Gód, to whom véngeance
be-*lóng*-cth, shéw thy^sélf.

2 Aríse, thou *Júdge* of the wórld : and rewárd
the próud after *their* de-sérv-ing.

3 Lórd, how lóng *shall* the^un-gód-ly : how
lóng shall the un-*gód*-ly trí-umph ?

4 How lóng shall áll wícked dóers spéak *so*
dis-daín^ful-ly : and máke *such* próud bóast-ing ?

5 They smíte down thy *péo*-ple, O Lórd : and
tróu-*ble* thine hé-ri^tage.

6 They múrder the wídow, *and* the strán-ger :
and put the *fá*-ther-less to^déath.

7 And yét they sáy, Túsh, the *Lórd* shall nót
see : neíther shall the Gód of Já-*cob* re-gárd it.

8 Take héed, ye unwíse a-*móng* the péople :
O ye fóols, whén *will* ye ún-der^stand ?

9 He that plánted the éar, *shall* he nót héar :
or hé that máde the éye, *shall* he nót see ?

10 Or hé that núrtur-*eth* the héa-then : it is hé
that téacheth man knówledge, shállt *not* he
pún-ish ?

11 The Lórd *knów*-eth^the thóughts^of mán :
that they áre but^vaín.

12 Bléssed is the mán whom thou *chá*-sten⁻est, O Lórd : and téachest *him* in thý láw ;

13 That thou mayest gíve him pátience in *time* of⌃ad-vér⁻si-ty : until the pít be dígged up for *the* un-gód-ly.

14 For the Lórd will not *fail* his péo-ple : neíther will he forsáke *his* in-hé-ri⁻tance ;

15 Until ríghteousness túrn agaín *un*-to júdge-ment : all súch as are trúe in *héart* shall fól-low⌃it.

16 Whó will ríse up with mé a-*gainst* the wíck-ed : or whó will táke my párt agaínst the *é*-vil-dó-ers ?

17 If the Lórd *had* not hélp⁻ed me : it hád not faíled but my sóul had been *put* to sí-lence.

18 But whén I saíd, My *fóot* hath slíp-ped : thy mércy, O Lórd, héld me⌃úp.

19 In the múltitude of the sórrows that I *had* in my héart : thy cómforts have re-*frésh*-ed my sóul.

20 Wílt thou have ány thing to dó with the *stóol* of wíck⁻ed-ness : which imágineth *mis*-chief as a⌃láw ?

21 They gáther them togéther agaínst the *sóul* of⌃the rígh-teous : and cóndemn the *in*-no-cent blóod.

22 But the Lórd *is* my ré-fuge : and my Gód is the stréngth *of* my cón-fi⁻dence.

23 He shall récompense them their wíckedness ; and destróy them in *their* own má-lice : yéa, the Lórd our Gód *shall* de-stróy thém.

Glóry be to the *Fá*-ther,⌃and to⌃the Són :
and *to* the Hó-ly⌃Ghóst.

As it wás in the begínning, is nów, and *év*-er
sháll be : wórld with-*óut* énd.   A-men.

THE 19th EVENING

PSALM 98   *Cantate Domino*   TONE III

O SÍNG unto the *Lórd* a néw sóng : for hé
hath done *mär*-vël-lous thíngs.

2 With his ówn right hánd, and *with* his⌃hó-ly
árm : hath he gótten him-*sélf* thë víc-to⌐ry.

3 The Lórd decláred *his* sal-vá-tion : his
ríghteousness hath he ópenly shéwed in the síght
öf thë héa-then.

4 He hath remémbered his mércy and trúth
towárd the *hóuse* of⌃Ís-ra-el : and áll the énds
of the wórld have séen the salvá-*tïon* öf óur Gód.

5 Shéw yourselves jóyful unto the *Lórd,* áll
ye lánds : síng, re-*joïce,* änd gíve thánks.

6 Praíse the *Lórd* up⌐ón the hárp : síng to the
hárp with a psálm *öf* thänks-gív-ing.

7 With trúmpets *al*-so, and sháwms : O shéw
yourselves jóyful be-*före* thë Lórd the⌃Kíng.

8 Let the séa make a noíse, and *áll* that⌃thére-in
is : the róund wórld, and *théy* thät dwéll there⌐ín.

9 Let the flóods cláp their hánds; and let the hílls be jóyful to-*gé*-ther^be^fóre the Lórd : for he is *cöme* tö júdge the^eárth.

10 With ríghteousness *shall* he^júdge the wórld : and the péo-*plë* wīth é-qui^ty.

Glóry b**e** to the *Fá*-ther,^and^to the Són : and *tö* thë Hó-ly^Ghóst.

As it wás in the begínning, is nów, and *év*-er sháll be : wórld with-*öut* ënd.   A-men.

PSALM 99   *Dominus regnavit*   TONE I

THE LÓRD is Kíng, be the péople néver
    so im-*pá*-tient : he sítteth betwéen the chérubims, be the éarth néver *so* un-qúi^et.

2 The Lórd is gréat in *Sý*-on : and hígh a-*bove* all péo^ple.

3 They shall give thánks únto *thy* Náme : which is gréat, wónder-*ful*, and hó^ly.

4 The Kíng's pówer loveth júdgement ; thou hast prepáred é-*qui*-ty : thou hast éxecuted júdgement and ríghteous-*ness* in Já^cob.

5 O mágnify the Lórd *our* Gód : and fall dówn befóre his fóotstool, for *he* is hó^ly.

6 Móses and Aáron amóng his príests ; **and** Sámuel among súch as cáll upon *his* Náme : these cálled upon the Lórd, *and* he héard^them.

7 He spáke unto them óut of the clóudy *píl*-lar : for they képt his téstimonies ; and the láw *that* he gáve⌃them.

8 Thou héardest them, O Lórd *our* Gód : thou forgávest them, O Gód ; and púnishedst their *ówn* in-vén⌐tions.

9 O mágnify the Lórd our Gód ; and wórship him upón his hó-*ly* híll : for the Lórd our *Gód* is hó⌐ly.

Glóry be to the Fáther, and to *the* Són : and *to* the Hó⌐ly⌃Ghóst.

As it wás in the begínning, is nów, and éver *sháll* be : wórld with-*óut* énd.   A⌐men.

PSALM 100   *Jubilate Deo*   TONE V

O BE jóyful in the Lórd, áll ye *lánds* : sérve the Lórd with gládness ; and cóme before his *pré*-sence with⌃a söng.

2 Be ye súre that the Lórd he is *Gód* : it is hé that hath máde us, and nót we oursélves ; we are his péople, and the *shéep* of his pás-türe.

3 O ᶢó your wáy into his gátes with thánks-giving, and into his cóurts with *práise* : be thánkful unto hím, and spéak *good* of his Näme.

4 For the Lórd is grácious ; his mércy is ever--*lást*-ing : and his trúth endúreth from generátion to *ge*-ne-rá-tïon.

Glóry be to the Fáther, and to the *Són* : and
to the Hó͟ly Ghöst.

As it wás in the begínning, is nów, and éver
sháll be : world with-*out* end.   A-mën.

PSALM 101   *Misericordiam et judicium*

1 My sóng shall be of mércy and *júdge*-ment :
unto thée, O *Lórd*, will I sĭng.

2 O lét me have únder-*stánd*-ing : in the *wáy*
of gód͟li-nëss.

3 Whén wilt thou cóme unto *mé* : I will wálk
in my hóuse *with* a pér͟fect hëart.

4 I will táke no wícked thing in hánd ; I háte
the síns of un-*faĭth*-ful͟ness : there shall nó such
cléave un-to më.

5 A fróward héart shall depárt from *mé* : I will
not knów a *wíck*-ed pér-sön.

6 Whóso prívily slándereth his *neĭgh*-bour :
hím will I^de-ströy.

7 Whóso hath álso a próud lóok and hígh
stó-mach : I *will* not súf͟fer hīm.

8 Mine éyes lóok upon súch as are faíthful in the
lánd : that *théy* may dwéll͟with më.

9 Whóso léadeth a gódly *lĭfe* : hé shall *be* my
sér-vänt.

10 There shall nó deceítful pérson dwéll in my
hóuse : he that télleth líes shall not *tár*-ry in my
sĭght.

11 I shall sóon destróy all the ungódly that are

ín the *lánd* : that I may róot out áll wícked dóers
from the *cí*-ty of⌢the Lörd.

Glóry be to the Fáther, and to the *Són* : and
to the Hó�"ly Ghöst.

As it wás in the begínning, is nów, and éver
sháll be : wórld with-*oút* énd.   A-mën.

THE 20th EVENING

P<small>SALM</small> 104   *Benedic anima mea*   T<small>ONE</small> VIII

PR'AISE THE Lórd, O my *sóul* : O Lórd
my Gód, thou art becóme excéeding
glórious ; thou art clóthed with májes-*ty* and
hó-nour.

2 Thou déckest thysélf with líght as it wére
with a *gár*-ment : and spréadest out the héavens
like a cúr-tain.

3 Who láyeth the béams of his chámbers in
the *wá*-ters : and máketh the clóuds his cháriot,
and wálketh upón the *wings* of the wínd.

4 He máketh his ángels *spí*-rits : and his
mínis-*ters* a flá-ming⌢fíre.

5 He laíd the foundátions of the *éarth* : that
it néver should *móve* at á-ny⌢tíme.

6 Thou cóveredst it with the déep líke as with
a *gár*-ment : the wáters *stánd* in the hílls.

7 At thý rebúke they *flée* : at the voíce of thy thún-*der* they áre a⌐fraíd.

8 They go úp as hígh as the hílls; and dówn to the válleys be-*néath* : éven unto the pláce which thou hast ap-*point*-ed for thém.

9 Thou hast sét them their bóunds which they sháll not *páss* : neíther túrn agaín to *cóv*-er the eárth.

10 He séndeth the spríngs ínto the *rí*-vers : which *rún* a-móng the⌒hílls.

11 All béasts of the fíeld drínk there-*óf* : and the wíld *áss*-es quénch their⌒thírst.

12 Besíde them shall the fówls of the aír have their hábi-*tá*-tion : and síng a-*móng* the brán-ches.

13 He wátereth the hílls from a-*bóve* : the eárth is fílled with the *frúit* of thy wórks.

14 He bríngeth forth gráss for the *cát*-tle : and gréen hérb for the *sér*-vice of mén ;

15 That he may bring fóod out of the eárth; and wíne that maketh glád the héart of *mán* : and oíl to máke him a chéerful cóuntenance ; and bréad to *stréngth*-en mán's héart.

16 The trées of the Lórd álso are fúll of *sáp* : éven the cédars of Líbanus which *hé* hath plán-ted ;

17 Whérein the bírds máke their *nésts* : and the fír-trees are a *dwéll*-ing for the⌒stórk.

18 The hígh hílls are a réfuge for the wíld *góats* : and só are the stóny rócks *for* the có-nies.

19 He appoínted the móon for cértain *séa*-sons :
and the sún knów-*eth* his gó-ing⌃dówn.

20 Thou mákest dárkness that it máy be *níght* :
wherein áll the béasts of the *fór*-est do móve.

21 The líons róaring áfter their *préy* : do *séek*
their méat from⌃Gód.

22 The sún aríseth, and they gét them awáy
to-*gé*-ther : and láy them *dówn* in theír déns.

23 Mán goeth fórth to his wórk, and to his
lá-bour : un-*tíl* the éve-ning.

24 O Lórd, how mánifold are thý *wórks* : in
wísdom hast thou máde them áll ; the eárth is
fúll *of* thy rích-es.

25 Só is the gréat and wíde sea *ál*-so : whereín are
thíngs créeping innúmerable, both *smáll* and gréat
beásts.

26 Thére go the shíps, and thére is thát Le-*ví*-a-⌃
-than : whom thóu hast máde to táke his *pás*-time
there-in.

27 These waít áll upón *thée* : that thou máyest
gíve them méat *in* dúe séa-son.

28 Whén thou gívest it thém they *gáth*-er⌃it :
and whén thou ópenest thy hánd they are *fíll*-ed
with góod.

29 Whén thou hídest thy fáce they are *tróu*-bled :
when thou tákest awáy their bréath they díe ;
and are túrned a-*gaín* to theír dúst.

30 Whén thou léttest thy bréath go fórth théy
shall be *máde* : and thóu shalt rénew the *fáce*
of the eárth.

F

31 The glórious Májesty of the Lórd shall endúre for *év*-er : the Lórd shall re-*joíce* in hís wórks.

32 The éarth shall trémble at the lóok of *hím* : if he dó but tóuch *the* hílls, théy shall⌢smóke.

33 I will síng unto the Lórd as lóng as I *líve* : I will praíse my Gód while I *háve* my bé-ing.

34 And só shall my wórds *pléase* hím : my jóy *shall* be ín the⌢Lórd.

35 As for sínners, they shall be consúmed óut of the éarth ; and the ungódly shall cóme to an *énd* : praíse thou the Lórd, O *my* sóul, praíse the⌢Lórd.

Glóry be to the Fáther, and to the *Són* : and *to* the Hó-ly⌢Ghóst.

As it wás in the begínning, is nów, and éver *sháll* be : wórld with-*óut* énd.   A-men.

THE 21st EVENING

PSALM 106   *Confitemini Domino*   TONE VI

O GIVE thánks unto the Lórd, for *he* is grá-cious : and his mércy endúr-*eth* för év-er.

2 Whó can expréss the nóble *ácts* of the Lórd : or *shéw* förth áll his⌢práise ?

3 Bléssed are théy that *ál*-way^keep júdge-ment :
and dö rígh-teous͡ness.

4 Remémber me, O Lórd, accórding to the
fávour that thou béarest ún-*to* thy péople : O
vísit me with *thý* säl-vá-tion ;

5 That I may sée the felícity *of* thy chó-sen :
and rejoíce in the gládness of thy péople ; and
give thánks with *thine* ïn-hé-ri͡tance.

6 We have sínned *with* our fá-thers : we have
dóne amíss, *and* dëalt wíck-ed͡ly.

7 Our fáthers regárded nót thy wónders in
'Egypt ; neíther képt they thy great góodness *in*
re-mém-brance : but were disobédient at the séa ;
éven *at* thë Réd séa.

8 Névertheless, he hélped them *for* his Náme's
sáke : that hé might máke his *pów*-ër to be^
knówn.

9 He rebúked the Réd séa álso, and *it* was
drí͡ed.up : so he léd them thróugh the déep, as
thróugh ä wíl-der͡ness.

10 And he sáved them fróm the *ád*-ver-sá͡ry's
hánd : and delívered them from the hánd *of*
thë é-ne͡my.

11 As for thóse that tróubled them, the wáters
ó-ver-whélm͡ed them : there was not *óne* öf
thém léft.

12 Thén be-*liev*-ed théy^his wórds : and sáng
praise ün-to him.

13 But withín a whíle *they* for-gát^his wórks :
and would nót a-*bíde* hïs cóun-sel.

14 But lúst came upón them *in* the wíl⸗der-ness :
and they témpted Gód *in* thë dé-sert.

15 And he *gáve* them theír^de-síre : and sent
léanness withál *in*-tö theír sóul.

16 They ángered Móses *al*-so in^the ténts : and
Aáron *the* saïnt of the^Lórd.

17 So the eárth opéned, and *swál*-lowed^up
Dá-than : and cóvered the congregátion *of*
Ä-bí-ram.

18 And the fíre was kíndled *in* their cóm⸗pa-ny :
the fláme burnt úp *the* ün-gód-ly.

19 They máde a *cálf* in Hó-reb : and wórshipped
the *mól*-tën í-mage.

20 Thús they *túrn*-ed^their gló-ry : into the
simílitude of a *cálf* thät éat-eth^háy.

21 And they forgát *Gód* their Sá-viour : who had
dóne so gréat *things* ïn 'E-gypt ;

22 Wóndrous wórks *in* the lánd^of Hám : and
féarful thíngs *by* thë Réd séa.

23 So he saíd, he wóuld have destróyed them ;
had not Móses his chósen stóod be-*fóre* him in^the
gáp : to túrn awáy his wráthful indignátion ; lést
he *shóuld* dë-stróy them.

24 Yéa, they thóught *scórn* of^that pléa⸗sant
lánd : and gáve no crédence *ún*-tö his wórd ;

25 But *múr*-mur⸗ed in^theír ténts : and héarkened
nót unto *the* voïce of the^Lórd.

26 Then líft he up his *hánd* a-gaínst them : to
overthrów them *in* thë wíl-der⸗ness ;

27 To cást out their séed a-*móng* the nátions :
and to scát-*ter* thëm in the⌢lánds.

28 They joíned themsélves unto *Bá*-al-pe-or :
and áte the óf-*fer*-ings of the⌢déad.

29 Thús they provóked him to ánger with their
ówn in-vén-tions : and the plágue was *gréat*
ä-mong them.

30 Thén stood up Phí-ne-*es* and práy-ed : and
so *the* plágue céas-ed.

31 And that was cóunted unto *him* for rígh⌐
teous-ness : among áll postéri-*ties* för év-er⌐more.

32 They ángered him álso at the *wá*-ters of
strífe : so that he púnished Mó-*ses* för theír sakes ;

33 Becáuse they pro-*vó*-ked⌢his spí-rit : so that
he spáke unadví-*sed*-lÿ with his⌢líps.

34 Neíther destróyed *they* the héa-then : as the
Lórd cöm-mánd-ed⌢them ;

35 But were míngled a-*móng* the héa-then : and
léarn-ëd theír wórks.

36 Iñsomuch that they wórshipped their ídols ;
which túrned *to* their ówn⌢de-cáy : yéa, they
óffered their sóns and their dáughters *un*-tö
dé-vils ;

37 And shéd ínnocent blóod ; éven the blóod of
their sóns and *of* their daúgh-ters : whom they
óffered unto the ídols of Cánaan ; and the lánd
was de-*fíl*-ëd with blóod.

38 Thús were they staíned *with* their ówn
wórks : and went a whóring with their *ówn*
ïn-vén-tions.

39 Thérefore was the wráth of the Lórd kíndled a-*gaínst* his péo-ple : ínsomuch that he abhórred his *ówn* ín-he-rí⁼tance.

40 And he gáve them óver into the *hánd* of^the héa-then : and they that háted them *were* lörds ó-ver^them.

41 Their éne-*mies* op-préss⁼ed them : and hád them *ín* süb-jéc-tion.

42 Mány a tíme did *he* de-lí⁻ver them : but they rebélled against him with their ówn invéntions ; and were bróught dówn *in* theïr wíck-ed⁼ness.

43 Névertheless, whén he sáw *their* ad-vér⁼si-ty : *he* hëard theír com⁼plaínt.

44 He thóught upon his cóvenant ; and pítied them, accórding unto the múltitude *of* his mér-cies : yéa, he máde all thóse that léd them away cáp-*tive* tö pí-ty^them.

45 Delíver us, O Lórd our Gód ; and gáther us from a-*móng* the héa-then : that we may gíve thánks unto thy hóly Náme ; and máke our *bóast* öf thý praíse.

46 Bléssed be the Lórd Gód of 'Israel from everlásting, and *wórld* with-óut énd : and let áll the péo-*ple* säy, A-men.

Glóry be to the *Fá*-ther,^and to^the Són : and *to* thë Hó-ly^Ghóst.

As it wás in the begínning, is nów, and *év*-er sháll be : wórld with-*óut* ënd.   A-men.

THE 22nd EVENING

PSALM 108   *Paratum cor meum*   TONE I

O GÓD, my héart is réady, my héart is
réa-dy : I will síng and give praíse with
the best mém-*ber* that Ï have.

2 Awáke, thou lúte, *and* hárp : I mysélf will
a-*wáke* right eär-ly.

3 I will give thánks unto thée, O Lórd, amóng
the *péo*-ple : I will sing praíses unto thée a-*móng*
the nä-tions.

4 For thy mércy is gréater than the *héa*-vens :
and thy trúth réacheth *un*-to thë clóuds.

5 Sét up thysélf, O Gód, abóve the *héa*-vens :
and thy glóry *a*-bóve äll the⌢eárth.

6 That thy belóved may be de-lí-*ver*-ed : let
thy ríght hand sáve *them*, and hëar thou⌢me.

7 Gód hath spóken in his hó-*li*-ness : I will
rejoíce therefore, and divíde Sýchem ; and mete
óut the vál-*ley* of Süc-coth.

8 Gílead is mine, and Manásses *is* míne :
'Ephraim álso is the *stréngth* of mÿ héad.

9 Júdah is my láw-giver ; Móab is my *wásh*-
pot : over 'Edom will I cást out my shóe ; upon
Philýstia *will* I trī-umph.

10 Whó will léad me ínto the stróng *cí*-ty : and
whó will bríng me *ín*-to Ë-dom ?

11 Hást not thóu forsáken us, O Gód : and wílt not thóu, O Gód, go *fórth* with öur hósts ?

12 O hélp us agaínst the é-*ne*-my : for vaín *is* the hëlp of^mán.

13 Through Gód we shall dó *great* ácts : and it is hé that shall tréad *dówn* our ë-ne⌢mies.

Glóry be to the Fáther, and to *the* Són : and *to* the Hö-ly^Ghóst.

As it wás in the begínning, is nów, and éver *sháll* be : wórld with-*óut* énd.   Ä-men.

PSALM 109   *Deus laudum*   TONE IV

H OLD NOT thy tóngue, O Gód *of* my práise : for the móuth of the ungódly ; yéa, the móuth of the deceítful is ó-*pen*-ed up-ón me.

2 And they have spóken agaínst me *with* fálse tóngues : they cómpassed me abóut álso with wórds of hátred ; and fóught a-*gaínst* me with-óut a^cáuse.

3 For the lóve that I hád unto thém ; ló, they take nów my cón-*tra*-ry párt : but I *give* my-self ún-to^práyer.

4 Thús have they rewárded me é-*vil* for góod : and há-*tred* for my góod wíll.

5 Sét thou an ungódly mán to be *rú*-ler ó-ver^ him : and let Sátan *stánd* at his ríght hánd.

6 When séntence is given upón him, lét him
be con-dém-ned : and lét his práyer *be* túrn-ed
ín-to͡sín.

7 Lét his *dáys* be féw : and lét anó-*ther* táke
his óf-fice.

8 Lét his chíl-*dren* be fá-ther͡less : and *his* wífe
a wí-dow.

9 Lét his chíldren be vágabonds, and *bég* their
bréad : lét them séek it álso out of *dé*-so-late
plá-ces.

10 Lét the extórtioner consúme áll *that* he háth :
and lét the strán-*ger* spoíl his lá-bour.

11 Lét there be nó *mán* to pí-ty͡hím : nor to
have compássion upon his *fá*-ther-less chíl-dren.

12 Lét his postérity *be* de-stróy-ed : and in the
néxt generátion lét *his* náme be cléan put͡óut.

13 Lét the wíckedness of his fáthers be hád in
remémbrance in the síght *of* the Lórd : and lét
not the sín of his *mó*-ther be dóne a͡wáy.

14 Lét them álway be be-*fóre* the Lórd : that
he may róot out the memórial *of* thém from óff
the͡éarth ;

15 And thát, becaúse his mínd was nót *to* dó
góod : but pérsecuted the póor hélpless mán ;
that he might sláy him that *was* véx-ed at the͡
héart.

16 His delíght was in cúrsing ; and it shall
háp-pen ún-to͡him : he lóved not bléssing ;
thérefore *shall* it be fár from͡him.

17 He clóthed himsélf with cúrsing, like as *with*

a raí-ment : and it shall cóme into his bówels like wáter, and *like* oíl in-to his^bónes.

18 Lét it be unto hím as the clóke that he *háth* up-ón him : and as the gírdle that he is ál-*way* gírd-ed with-al.

19 Lét it thus háppen from the Lórd ún-*to* mine é-ne^mies : and to thóse that spéak *é*-vil a-gaínst my^sóul.

20 But déal thou with mé, O Lórd Gód, ac-córding ún-*to* thy Náme : for *swéet* is thy mér-cy.

21 O delíver me, for I am hélp-*less* and póor : and my héart is *wóund*-ed with-ín me.

22 I go hénce like the shádow *that* de-párt-eth : and am dríven a-*wáy* as the gráss-hop^per.

23 My knées are *wéak* through fást-ing : my flésh is dríed up *for* wánt of fát-ness.

24 I becáme álso a repróach *un*-to thém : théy that lóoked upon *me* shá-ked their héads.

25 Hélp me, O *Lórd* my Gód : O sáve me accórd-*ing* to thy mér-cy ;

26 And théy shall knów, how that thís *is* thý hánd : and that *thŏu*, Lórd, hast dóne it.

27 Thóugh they cúrse, *yet* bléss thóu : and lét them be confóunded that ríse up agaínst me ; but *lét* thy sér-vant re^joíce.

28 Let mine ádversaries be clóth-*ed* with sháme : and lét them cóver themsélves with their ówn con-*fú*-sion, as with a^clóke.

29 'As for me, I will gíve great thánks unto the

Lórd *with* my móuth : and praíse him *a*-móng
the múl-ti̭ctude ;

30 For hé shall stánd at the ríght hánd *of* the
póor : to sáve his sóul from *un*-rígh-teous júd-ges.

Glóry be to the Fáther, and *to* the Són : *and*
to the Hó-ly⌢Ghóst.

As it wás in the begínning, is nów, and *év*-er
sháll be : wórld *with*-óut énd.   A-men.

THE 23rd EVENING

Psalm 114   *In exitu Israel*   Peregrine Tone

WHĔN 'Israel came *óut* of 'E-gypt : ÄND
the hóuse of Jácob from amóng the
stránge péo-plë,

2 Júdah was his *sánc*-tu-a-ry : and 'Israel his
do-mín-ïon.

3 The séa *saw* thát, and fléd : Jórdan *was* drí̭cven
bäck.

4 The móuntains *skíp*-ped like ráms : and the
líttle hílls *like* yóung shëep.

5 What aíleth thee, O thou séa, *that* thou
fléd-dest : and thou Jórdan, that thóu *wast*
drí̭cven bäck ?

6 Ye móuntains, that ye *skíp*-ped like ráms :
and ye líttle hílls, *like* yóung shëep ?

7 Trémble, thou éarth, at the *pré*-sence of the⌢
Lórd : at the présence of the Gód *of* Já-cöb ;

8 Who túrned the hárd róck into a *stánd*-ing wá-ter : and the flínt-stone ínto *a* spríng‿ing wëll.

Glóry be to the Fá-*ther*, and to the‿Són : and to *the* Hó‿ly Ghöst.

As it wás in the begínning, is nów, and *év*-er shǎll be : wórld withóut *énd.* A-mën.

PSALM 115   *Non nobis Domine*   TONE V

NOT UN-to ús, O Lórd, nót unto ús ; but unto thý Náme give the *praise* : for thy lóving mércy, and *for* thy trúth's sáke.

2 Whérefore shall the héathen *sáy* : *Whére* is nów their‿Gód ?

3 As for óur Gód, he is in *héa*-ven : he hath dóne whatso-*év*-er pléas-ed‿hím.

4 Their ídols are sílver and *góld* : éven the *wórk* of mén's hánds.

5 They have móuths, and *spéak* not : éyes have *théy*, and sée not.

6 They have eárs, and *héar* not : nóses have *théy*, and sméll not.

7 They have hánds, and hándle not ; féet have théy, and *wálk* not : neíther *spéak* they thróugh their‿thróat.

8 They that máke them are líke *un*-to‿thém : and só are áll súch as *put* their trúst in‿thém.

9 But thóu, hoúse of 'Israel, trúst thou in the *Lórd* : he is their *súc*-cour and de⌐fence.

10 Ye hóuse of 'Aaron, pút your trúst in the *Lórd* : he is their hélper *and* de-fénd-er.

11 Ye that féar the Lórd, pút your trúst in the *Lórd* : he is their hélper *and* defénd-er.

12 The Lórd hath been míndful of ús, and hé shall *bléss* us : even hé shall bléss the hóuse of 'Israel; he shall bléss the *house* of A-aron.

13 He shall bléss thém that féar the *Lórd* :— both smáll and⌒gréat.

14 The Lórd shall incréase you móre and *móre :* yóu *and* your chíl-dren.

15 Yé are the bléssed of the *Lórd* : who máde *héa*-ven and éarth.

16 'All the whóle héavens are the *Lórd's* : the éarth hath he gíven to the *chíl*-dren of mén.

17 The déad praíse not thée, O *Lórd* : neíther all théy that go dówn *in*-to sí-lence.

18 But wé will praíse the *Lórd* : from thís time fórth for ev-*er*-more.   Praise the⌒Lord.

   Glóry be to the Fáther, and to the *Són* : and *to* the Hó-ly⌒Ghóst.

   As it wás in the begínning, is nów, and éver *shall* be : wórld with-*out* énd.   A-men.

THE 24th EVENING

PSALM 119   *Beati immaculati*   TONE III

BLÉSSED are thóse that are únde-*ft*-led⌃
in the wáy : and wálk in the láw *of* the
Lörd.

2 Bléssed are théy that kéep his *tés*-ti-mo-nies :
and séek him wíth *their* whóle hëart.

3 For théy who *dó* no⌃wíck-ed-ness : wálk *in* his
wäys.

4 *Thóu* hast chár-ged : that we shall díligently
kéep thy *com*-mánd-mënts.

5 O that my *wáys* were⌃made⌃só di-réct : that
I might kéep *thy* stá-tütes !

6 So shall I *nót* be⌃con-fóund-ed : while I have
respéct unto áll thy *com*-mánd-mënts.

7 I will thánk thee *with* an⌃un⌐feígn-ed héart :
when I shall have léarned the júdgements of
thy rígh⌐teous-nëss.

8 I will kéep thy *cé*-re-mo-nies : O forsáke me
not út⌐ter-lÿ.

Glóry be to the *Fá*-ther,⌃and⌃to the Són : and
to *the* Hó⌐ly Ghöst.

As it wás in the begínning, is nów, and *év*-er
sháll be : wórld withóut *énd*.   A-mën.

In quo corriget

9 Whérewithál shall a *yóung* mán^cléanse his wáy : éven by rúling himself áf-*ter* thy wörd.

10 With my whóle héart *have* I sóught thee : O let me nót go wróng out of thý *com*-mánd--ments.

11 Thy wórds have I *hid* with⌒ín my héart : that I shóuld not sín *a*-gaínst thëe.

12 *Bléss*-ed^art^thóu, O Lórd : O téach me *thy* stá-tütes.

13 With my líps have *I* been téll-ing : of áll the júdgements *of* thy möuth.

14 I have hád as gréat delíght in the wáy of thy *tés*-ti-mo-nies : as in all mánner *of* rich-ës.

15 I will tálk of *thy* com-mánd-ments : and have respéct un-*to* thy wäys.

16 My delíght shall bé *in* thy stá-tutes : and I will nót *for*-gét^thy wörd.

Glóry be to the *Fá*-ther,^and^to the Són : and to *the* Hó⌒ly Ghöst.

As it wás in the begínning, is nów, and *év*-er shall be : wórld withóut *énd*. A-mën.

Retribue servo tuo Tone VIII

O DO wéll unto thy *sér*-vant : that I may *live*, and kéep^thy^wórd.

18 'Open thóu mine *éyes* : that I may sée the wóndrous *things* of thý^láw.

19 I am a stránger upon *eárth* : O híde not thy com-*mánd*-ments fróm^me.

20 My sóul bréaketh óut for the véry férvent de-*síre* : that it hath álway ún-*to* thy júdge⌐ments.

21 Thóu hast rebúked the *próud* : and cúrsed are théy that do érr from *thy* com-mánd⌐ments.

22 O túrn from me sháme and re-*búke* : for I have képt thy *tés*-ti-mo⌐nies.

23 Prínces álso did sít and spéak a-*gaínst* me : but thy sérvant is óccupied *in* thy stá⌐tutes.

24 For thy téstimonies are my de-*líght* : *and* my cóun⌐sel⌐lors.

Glóry be to the Fáther, and to the *Són* : and *to* the Hó⌐ly^Ghóst.

As it wás in the begínning, is nów, and éver *shátt* be : wórld with-*óut* énd. A⌐men.

Adhæsit pavimento

25 My sóul cléaveth to the *dúst* : O quícken thou me, accórd-*ing* to thý^wórd.

26 I have acknówledged my wáys, and thou *héard*-est^me : O téach *me* thy stá⌐tutes.

27 Máke me to understánd the wáy of thy com-*mánd*-ments : and só shall I tálk *of* thy wón⌐drous^wórks.

28 My sóul mélteth awáy for véry *héa*-vi⌐ness : cómfort thou me accórding *un*-to thý^wórd.

29 Táke from me the wáy of *lý*-ing : and caúse thou me to máke *múch* of thý^láw.

30 I have chósen the wáy of *trúth* : and thy
júdgements have I *laíd* be-fóre˘me.

31 I have stúck unto thy testi-*mó*-nies : O *Lórd,*
con-fóund˘me˘nót.

32 I will rún the wáy of thy com-*mánd*-ments :
when thou hast sét my *héart* at lí˘ber˘ty.

   Glóry be to the Fáther, and to the *Són* : and
to the Hó˘ly˘Ghóst.

   As it wás in the begínning, is nów, and éver
sháll be : wórld with-*óut* énd.   A˘men.

THE 25th EVENING

Manus tuæ fecerunt me   Tone VII

THY HÁNDS have máde me and *fá*-shion-ed
me : O gíve me understánding ; that I
may léarn *thy* com-mánd-ments.

74 They that féar thee will be *glád* when˘they
sée me : becáuse I have pút my *trúst* in thý wórd.

75 I knów, O Lórd, that thy *júdge*-ments are
ríght : and that thóu of very faíthfulness hast
cáused me *to* be tróu-bled.

76 O lét thy mérciful kíndness *be* my cómfort : accórding to thy wórd un-*to* thy sér-vant.

77 O lét thy lóving mércies come unto *mé*, that
I˘may líve : for thy *láw* is my de˘líght.

78 Let the próud be confóunded ; for they go

G

wíckedly a-*bóut* to^de-stróy me : but I will be
óccupied in *thý* com-mánd-ments.

79 Let súch as féar thee, and have knówn thy
tés-ti-mo-nies : be *túrn*-ed un-to^me.

80 O lét my héart be *sóund* in^thy stá-tutes :
that I be *nót* a-shám-ed.

Glóry be to the *Fá*-ther,^and to^the Són : and
to the Hó-ly^Ghóst.

As it wás in the begínning, is nów, and *év*-er
sháll be : wórld with-*óut* énd.   A-men.

Defecit anima mea

81 My sóul hath lónged for *thý* sal-vá-tion : and
I have a góod hópe be-*cáuse* of thy wórd.

82 Mine éyes long *sóre* for thy wórd : sáying,
O whén *wilt* thou cóm-fort^me ?

83 For I am becóme like a *bót*-tle in^the smóke :
yét do I nót for-*gét* thy stá-tutes.

84 Hów mány are the *dáys* of^thy sér-vant : whén
wilt thóu be avénged of thém that *pér*-se-cute
me ?

85 The próud have *díg*-ged píts^for me : which
áre not *áf*-ter thy láw.

86 'All thy com-*mánd*-ments are trúe : they
pérsecute me fálsely ; O be thóu my^hélp.

87 They had álmost made an énd of *me* up-ón
eárth : but I forsóok not *thy* com-mánd-ments.

88 O quícken me áfter thy *lóv*-ing-kínd-ness :
and só shall I kéep the tésti-*mo*-nies^of thý
móuth.

Glóry be to the *Fá*-ther,⌢and to⌢the Són :
and *to* the Hó-ly⌢Ghóst.

As it wás in the begínning, is nów, and *év*-er
sháll be : wórld with-*óut* énd.   A-men.

In æternum Domine   Tone I

O LÓRD, thy wórd : endúreth for év-*er*
in hëa-vën.

90 Thy trúth also remáineth from óne generátion
to a-*nó*-ther : thóu hast laíd the foundátion of
the eárth, and *it* a-bĭ-dëth.

91 They contínue this dáy accórding to thine
ór-*di*-nance : for *áll* things sërve thëe.

92 If my delíght had not béen in *thy* láw : I
should have pérished *in* my tröu-blë.

93 I will néver forgét thy com-*mánd*-ments :
for with thém thou hast *quíck*-en-ëd më.

94 I am thíne, O *sáve* me : for I have sóught *thy*
com-mänd-mënts.

95 The ungódly laid waít for me to de-*stróy*
me : but I will consíder thy *tés*-ti-mö-nïes.

96 I sée that áll things cóme to *an* énd : but thy
commándment *is* ex-cëed-ing⌢bröad.

Glóry be to the Fáther, and to *the* Són : and
to the Hö-ly⌢Ghöst.

As it wás in the begínning, is nów, and éver
sháll be : wórld with-*óut* énd.   Ä-mën.

Quomodo dilexi

97 Lórd, what lóve have I únto *thy* láw : áll the
day lóng is my *stú*-dy ĭn īt.

98 Thóu through thy commándments hast máde
me wíser than mine é-*ne*-mies : for théy are
év-er wĭth më.

99 I have móre understánding than my *téach*-ers :
for thy téstimonies *are* my stü-dÿ.

100 I am wíser than the *á*-ged : because I kéep
thy com-mänd-mënts.

101 I have refraíned my féet from évery é-*vil*
wáy : that *I* may kĕep thy⌢wörd.

102 I have nót shrúnk from thy *júdge*-ments :
for thou teäch-est⌢më.

103 O how swéet are thy wórds únto *my* thróat :
yéa, swéeter than hóney *un*-to mÿ mōuth.

104 Thróugh thy commándments I get under-
-*stánd*-ing : thérefore I *háte* all ë-vil⌢wäys.

Glóry be to the Fáther, and to *the* Són : and
to the Hö-ly⌢Ghöst.

As it wás in the begínning, is nów, and éver
sháll be : wórld with-*óut* énd.   Ä-mën.

THE 26th EVENING

Clamavi in toto corde meo   Tone IV

I CÁLL with *my* whóle héart : héar me, O
Lórd, I *will* kéep thy stá-tutes.

146 Yéa, éven unto thée *do* I cáll : hélp me, and I shall kéep *thy* tés-ti-mo-nies.

147 Eárly in the mórning do I crý *un*-to thée : for ín *thy* wórd is mý trúst.

148 Mine éyes prevént *the* night-watch-es : that 'I might be óccu-*pi*-ed in thý wórds.

149 Héar my voíce, O Lórd, accórding unto thy *lóv*-ing-kínd-ness : quícken me, ac-*córd*-ing as thóu^art wónt.

150 They draw nígh that of málice *pér*-se-cute me : and *are* fár from thý láw.

151 Be thou nígh at *hánd*, O Lórd : for áll thy *com*-mánd-ments are trúe.

152 As concérning thy téstimonies, I **have** *knówn* long sínce : that thou hast gróund-*ed* thém for év-er.

Glóry be to the Fáther, and *to* the Són : *and* to the Hó^ly Ghóst.

As it wás in the begínning, is nów, and *év*-er sháll be : wórld *with*-óut énd.   A-men.

Vide humilitatem

153 O consíder mine advérsity, *and* delí-ver^ me : for I *do* nót for-gét^thy láw.

154 Avénge thou my cáuse, *and* de-lí-ver^me : quícken me, ac-*córd*-ing to thý wórd.

155 Héalth is fár from *the* un-gód-ly : for théy re-*gárd* not thy stá-tutes.

156 Gréat is thy mér-*cy*, O Lórd : quíck-*en* me, as thóu^art wónt.

157 Mány there áre that tróuble me, and *pér*-se-cute me : yét do I not swérve from *thy* tés-ti-mo-nies.

158 It gríeveth me when I sée *the* trans-grés-sors : becáuse *they* kéep not thý láw.

159 Consíder, O Lórd, how I lóve *thy* com- -mánd-ments : O quícken me, accórding to *thy* lóv-ing-kínd-ness.

160 Thy wórd is trúe from *év*-er-lást-ing : áll the júdgements of thy ríghteousness *en*-dúre for év⌐er-more.

    Glóry be to the Fáther, and *to* the Són : *and* to the Hó⌐ly Ghóst.

    As it wás in the begínning, is nów, aṅd *év*-er shall be : wórld *with*-óut énd.   A-men.

Principes persecuti sunt   TONE VI

PRÍNCES have pérsecuted *me* with-óut⌐a cáuse : but my héart stándeth in *áwe* öf thý wórd.

162 I am as *glád* of thy wórd : as óne that *find*-ëth gréat spóils.

163 As for líes, I *háte* and⌐ab-hór them : but thy *láw* dö I lóve.

164 Séven times a *dáy* do⌐I praíse thee : becáuse of thy *righ*-tëous júdge-ments.

165 Gréat is the péace that they *have* who lóve⌐ thy láw : and they are nót of-*fénd*-ëd at it.

166 Lórd, I have lóoked *for* thy sá⌒ving héalth :
and done áfter *thy* cöm-mánd-ments.

167 My sóul hath képt thy *tés*-ti-mo-nies : and
lóved *them* ëx-céed-ing⌒ly.

168 I have képt thy commándments and
tés-ti-mo-nies : for áll my wáys *are* bë-fóre thée.

Glóry be to the *F á*-ther,⌒and to⌒the Són : and
to thë Hó-ly⌒Ghóst.

As it wás in the begínning, is nów, and
év-er shÁll be : wórld with-*óut* ënd. A-men.

Appropinquet deprecatio

169 Let my cómplaint come be-*fóre* thee, O
Lórd : give me understánding, accórd-*ing* tö
thý wórd.

170 Let my supplicátion *come* be-fóre thée :
delíver me, accórd-*ing* tö thý wórd.

171 My líps shall *spéak* of thy praíse : when thou
hast táught *me* thÿ stá-tutes.

172 Yéa, my tóngue shall *sing* of thy wórd : for
áll thy commánd-*ments* äre rígh-teous.

173 Let *thine* hánd hélp me : for I have chósen
thy cöm-mánd-ments.

174 I have lónged for thy *sá*-ving héalth,⌒O
Lórd : and in thy *láw* ïs my de⌒líght.

175 O lét my sóul líve, and *it* shall praíse thee :
and thy júdge-*ments* shÄll hélp me.

176 I have góne astráy like a *shéep* that is lóst : O
séek thy sérvant ; for I do nót forgét *thy* cöm-
mánd-ments.

Glóry be to the *Fá*-ther,⌃and to⌃the Són :
and *to* thë Hó-ly⌃Ghóst.

As it wás in the begínning, is nów, and *év*-er
shǻll be : wórld with-*óut* ënd.   A-men.

THE 27th EVENING

W HÉN   THE   Lórd   túrned   agaín   the
captívi-*ty* of Sý-on : thén were we líke
un-*to* thém that⌃dréam.

2 Thén was our móuth *fill*-ed⌃with láugh-ter :
and *our* tóngue with⌃jóy.

3 Thén said théy a-*móng* the héa-then : The
Lórd hath done gréat *things* for thém.

4 Yéa, the Lórd hath done gréat thíngs for
ús al-réa-dy : whére-*of* we re⌃joíce.

5 Túrn our cap-*ti*-vi⌃ty, O Lórd : as the rí-*vers*
in the⌃sóuth.

6 *Théy* that sów in téars : *shall* réap in⌃jóy.

7 He that nów góeth on his wáy wéeping, and
béar-eth⌃forth góod séed : shall dóubtless come
agaín with jóy, and bríng *his* shéaves with⌃him.

Glóry be to the *Fá*-ther,⌃and⌃to the Són :
and to *the* Hó-ly⌃Ghóst.

As it wás in the begínning, is nów, and *év*-er
shǻll be : wórld withóut *énd*.   A-men.

PSALM 127   *Nisi Dominus*   TONE VII

EXCEPT the *Lórd* buíld the hóuse : their lábour is but *lóst* that buíld it.

2 Except the Lórd *kéep* the cí-ty ┆ the wátch-man *wák*-eth büt in⁀vaín.

3 It ís but lóst lábour that ye háste to ríse up éarly, and so láte take rést ; and éat the *bréad* of cáre⌢ful-ness : for só he gíveth *his* be-löv-ed⁀ sléep.

4 Ló, chíldren and the *frúit* of the wómb : are an héritage and gíft that *cóm*-eth öf the⁀Lórd.

5 Líke as the árrows in the *hánd* of⁀the gí-ant : even só are *the* yóung chĭl-dren.

6 Háppy is the mán that hath his *quí*-ver fúll⁀of thém : they shall nót be ashámed when they spéak with their *é*-ne⌢mies ĭn the⁀gáte.

Glóry be to the *Fá*-ther,⁀and to⁀the Són : and *to* the Hö-ly⁀Ghóst.

As it wás in the begínning, is nów, and *év*-er sháll be : wórld with-*óut* énd.   Ä-men.

PSALM 128   *Beati omnes*

1 Bléssed are áll *they* that féar⁀the Lórd : and *wálk* in hĭs wáys.

2 For thóu shalt éat the *lá*-bours⁀of thíne hánds : O wéll is thée, and *háp*-py shält thou⁀bé.

3 Thy wífe shall bé *as* the fruít⌒ful víne : upón the *wálls* of thīne hóuse.

4 Thy chíldren like the ó-live bránch-es : róund a-*bóut* thy tä-ble,

5 Ló, thús shall the *mán* be bléss-ed : that *féar*-eth thë Lórd.

6 The Lórd from out of Sýon *shall* so bléss thée : that thóu shalt see Jerúsalem in prospérity *all* thy lífe lóng.

7 Yéa, that thóu shalt sée thy *chíl*-dren's chíl-dren : and *péace* up⌒on 'Is̈-ra⌒el.

Glóry be to the *Fá*-ther,⌒and to⌒the Són : and *to* the Hö-ly⌒Ghóst.

As it wás in the begínning, is nów, and *év*-er sháll be : wórld with-*óut* énd.   Ä-men.

PSALM 129   *Sæpe expugnaverunt*   TONE II

MANY a tíme have they fóught against me írom my yóuth *úp* : may 'Is-*rä*-ël nów sáy.

2 Yéa, mány a tíme have they véxed me from my yóuth *úp* : but théy have nót prevaíl-*ĕd* ä-gaínst me.

3 The plówers plówed upón my *báck* : and *mäde* löng fúr-rows.

4 But the ríghteous *Lórd* : hath héwn the snáres of the ungód-*lÿ* īn píe-ces.

5 Lét them be confóunded and túrned *báck-*
-ward: as mány as have évil *wĭll* ät Sý-on.

6 Let them be éven as the gráss grówing upon
the *hóuse*-tops : which wíthereth afóre *ĭt* bĕ
plúck⌐ed up ;

7 Whereof the mówer fílleth nót his *hánd* :
neíther hé that bíndeth up the *shĕaves* hĭs
bó-som.

8 So that théy who go by sáy not so múch as;
The Lórd *prós*-per^you : we wísh you good lúck
in *thĕ* Näme of^the Lórd.

Glóry be to the Fáther, and to the *Són* : **and**
tŏ thë Hó⌐ly Ghóst.

As it wás in the begínning, is nów, and éver
shăll be : wórld with-*ŏut* ënd.   A-men.

PSALM 130   *De profundis*   TONE IV

ÓUT OF the déep have I cálled unto *thée,*
O O Lórd : Lórd, héar *my* voíce.

2 O lét thine éars con-*sĭ*-der wéll : the voíce
of my *com*-plaínt.

3 If thóu, Lórd, wilt be extréme to márk what
is *dóne* a-míss : O Lórd, whó may a-*bíde* it ?

4 For there is mér-*cy* with thée : thérefore shalt
thóu be *féar*-ed.

5 I lóok for the Lórd ; my sóul doth *wait*
for hím : in his wórd is *my* trúst.

6 My sóul fléeth ún-*to* the Lórd : befóre the mórning wátch, I sáy, befóre the mórn-*ing* wátch.

7 O 'Israel, trúst in the Lórd; for with the Lórd *there* is mér-cy : and with hím is plénteous re-*démp*-tion.

8 And hé shall *re*-déem 'Is-ra-el : from áll *his* síns.

Glóry be to the Fáther, and *to* the Són : and to the Hó-*ly* Ghóst.

As it wás in the begínning, is nów, and *év*-er sháll be : wórld withóut énd. *A*-men.

PSALM 131   *Domine non est*

1 Lórd, I am *nót* high-mínd-ed : I have no *próud* looks.

2 I dó not exércise mysélf *in* gréat mát-ters : which are tóo hígh *for* mé.

3 But I refraín my sóul, and kéep it lów; like as a chíld that is wéaned *from* his mó-ther : yéa, my sóul is éven as a wéan-*ed* chíld.

4 O Ísrael, trúst *in* the Lórd : from thís time fórth for év-*er*-more.

Glóry be to the Fáther, and *to* the Són : and to the Hó-*ly* Ghóst.

As it wás in the begínning, is nów, and *év*-er sháll be : wórld withóut énd. *A*-men.

THE 28th EVENING

PSALM 136   *Confitemini*   TONE V

O GIVE thánks unto the Lórd, for he is
    grá-cious : and his mércy en-*dúr*-eth for
év-er.

2 O give thánks unto the Gód of all *góds* : for
his mércy en-*dúr*-eth for év-er.

3 O thánk the Lórd of all *lórds* : for his mércy
en-*dúr*-eth for év-er.

4 Who ónly dóeth great *wón*-ders : for his mércy
en-*dúr*-eth for év-er.

5 Who by his éxcellent wísdom máde the
héa-vens : for his mércy en-*dúr*-eth for év-er.

6 Who laíd out the eárth above the *wá*-ters :
for his mércy en-*dúr*-eth for év-er.

7 Who hath máde great *líghts* : for his mércy
en-*dúr*-eth for év-er ;

8 The sún to rúle the *dáy* : for his mércy
en-*dúr*-eth for év-er ;

9 The móon and the stárs to góvern the *níght* :
for his mércy en-*dúr*-eth for év-er.

10 Who smóte Égypt with their *fírst*-born : for
his mércy en-*dúr*-eth for év-er ;

11 And bróught out Ísrael from a-*móng* them :
for his mércy en-*dúr*-eth for év-er ;

12 With a míghty hánd, and strétched out
árm : for his mércy en-*dúr*-eth for év-er.

13 Who divíded the Réd séa in twó *parts* : for
his mércy en-*dúr*-eth for év-er ;

14 And made 'Ísrael to gó through the *midst*
of^it : for his mércy en-*dúr*-eth for év-er.

15 But as for Pháraoh and his hóst ; he over-
thréw them in the Réd *séa* : for his mércy
en-*dúr*-eth for év-er.

16 Who léd his péople through the *wil*-der-ness :
for his mércy en-*dúr*-eth for év-er.

17 Who smóte great *kings* : for his mércy
en-*dúr*-eth for év-er ;

18 Yéa, and sléw míghty *kings* : for his mércy
en-*dúr*-eth for év-er ;

19 Séhon kíng of the *A*-mor-ites : for his mércy
en-*dúr*-eth for év-er ;

20 And 'Og the kíng of *Bá*-san : for his mércy
en-*dúr*-eth for év-er ;

21 And gáve away their lánd for an *hé*-ri-tage :
for his mércy en-*dúr*-eth for év-er ;

22 Even for an héritage unto Ísrael his *sér*-vant :
for his mércy en-*dúr*-eth for év-er.

23 Who remémbered us when we wére in
tróu-ble : for his mércy en-*dúr*-eth for év-er ;

24 And hath delívered us from our *é*-ne-mies :
for his mércy en-*dúr*-eth for év-er.

25 Who gíveth fóod to áll *flésh* : for his mércy
en-*dúr*-eth for év-er.

26 O give thánks unto the Gód of *héa*-ven : for
his mércy en-*dúr*-eth for év-er.

27 O give thánks unto the Lórd of *lórds* : for
his mércy en-*dúr*-eth for év-er.

Glóry be to the Fáther, and to the *Són* : and
to the Hó-ly^Ghóst.

As it wás in the begínning, is nów, and éver
shall be : wórld with-*óut* énd.   A-men.

PSALM 137   *Super flumina*   TONE I

B Y THE wáters of Bábylon we sát dówn
and wépt : when we remémbered *thée*, O
Sÿ-on.

2 As for our hárps, we hánged *them* úp : upón
the *trées* that arë^there-in.

3 For théy that léd us awáy cáptive requíred
of us thén a sóng ; and mélody in our héa-*vi*-ness :
Síng us óne of the *sóngs* of Sÿ-on.

4 Hów shall we síng the *Lórd's* sóng : *in* a
stränge lánd ?

5 If I forgét thee, O Jerú-*sa*-lem : lét my ríght
hánd for-*gét* her cün-ning.

6 If I do nót remémber thee ; lét my tóngue
cléave to the róof of *my* móuth : yéa, if I prefér
not Jerú-*sa*-lem ïn^my mírth.

7 Remémber the chíldren of 'Edom, O Lórd,
in the dáy of Jerú-*sa*-lem : how they saíd ; Dówn
with it, dówn with it, *é*-ven tö^the gróund.

8 O dáughter of Bábylon, wásted with mí-*se*-ry :
yéa, háppy shall he bé that rewardeth thee, as
thóu hast sërv⁀ed ús.

9 Bléssed shall he bé that táketh thy *chíl*-dren :
and thróweth *thém* a-gaïnst⁀the stónes.

  Glóry be to the Fáther, and to *the* Són : and
to the Hö⁀ly Ghóst.

  As it wás in the begínning, is nów, and éver
shâll be : wórld with-*óut* énd.   Ä-men.

PSALM 138   *Confitebor tibi*   TONE VI

I WILL give thánks unto thée, O Lórd, *with*
my whóle héart : éven before the góds will
I sing *praíse* ün-to thee.

  2 I will wórship towárd thy hóly témple ; and
praíse thy Náme, becáuse of thy lóving-*kínd*-ness
and trúth : for thou hast mágnified thy Náme,
and thy Wórd, *a*-böve áll thíngs.

  3 When I cálled upon *thée*, thou héard⁀est mé :
and endúedst my *sóul* wïth múch stréngth.

  4 All the kíngs of the eárth shall *praíse* thee, O
Lórd : for they have héard the *wórds* öf thý
móuth.

  5 Yéa, they shall síng in the *wáys* of the Lórd :
that gréat is the *gló*-rÿ of the⁀Lórd.

  6 For thóugh the Lórd be hígh, yet hath he
respéct *ún*-to⁀the lów-ly : as for the próud, he
behóldeth *them* ä-fár óff.

7 Thóugh I wálk in the mídst of tróuble ; yet shalt *thóu* re-frésh me : thou shalt strétch forth thy hánd upon the fúriousness of mine énemies ; and thy ríght *hánd* sh äll sáve me.

8 The Lórd shall make góod his lóving-*kínd-ness*^to-wárd me : yéa, thy mércy, O Lórd, endúreth for éver ; despíse not then the wórks *of* thīne ówn hánds.

Glóry be to the *Fá*-ther,^and to^the Són : and *to* thë Hó-ly^Ghóst.

As it wás in the begínning, is nów, and *év*-er sháll be : wórld with-*óut* ënd.   A-men.

THE 29th EVENING

PSALM 142   *Voce mea ad Dominum*   TONE II

I CRÍ-ed unto the Lórd with my *voíce* : yéa, éven unto the Lórd did I máke my súp-*pli*-ca-tion.

2 I póured óut my compláints be-*fóre* him : and shéwed him of *my* tróu-ble.

3 When my spírit was in héaviness thou knéwest my *páth* : in the wáy whereín I wálked have they prívily laíd *a* snáre^for mé.

4 I lóoked álso upón my ríght *hánd* : and sáw there was nó man thát *would* knów me.

5 I had no pláce to *flée* un÷to : and nó man cáred *for* mý sóul.

H

6 I críed unto thée, O Lórd, and *said* : Thóu art my hópe, and my pórtion in the lánd of *the* lív-ing.

7 Consíder my com-*plaint* : for I am *bróught* vé⌢ry lów.

8 O delíver me from my pér-se-*cu*-tors : for théy are *tóo* stróng⌢for mé.

9 Bríng my sóul out of príson; that I may give thánks únto thy *Náme* : which thíng if thou wilt gránt me; thén shall the ríghteous resórt unto *my* cóm⌢pa-ny.

Glóry be to the Fáther, and to the *Són* : and to *the* Hó⌢ly Ghóst.

As it wás in the begínning, is nów, and éver *shall* be : wórld withóut *énd*.   A-men.

PSALM 143   *Domine exaudi*   TONE III

H EAR MY práyer, O Lórd, and con-*sid*-er⌢ my de-síre : héarken unto me for thy trúth and rígh-*teous*-ness' säke.

2 And énter nót into júdgement *with* thy sér-vant : for in thý síght shall nó man líving be jús-*ti*-fi-ëd.

3 For the énemy hath pérsecuted my sóul; he hath smítten my life *dówn* to the gróund : he hath laíd me in the dárkness; as the mén that háve *been* long dëad.

4 Thérefore is my spírit *véx*-ed^with-ín me :
and my héart withín me *is* dé꞊so-läte.

5 Yét do I remémber the tíme pást ; I *múse*
up꞊on^áll thy wórks : yéa, I éxercise mysélf in
the wórks *of* thy händs.

6 I strétch fórth my *hánds* un-to thée : my
sóul gáspeth unto thée as *a* thír꞊sty länd.

7 Héar me, O Lórd, and that sóon ; for my
spí-rit^wáx-eth faínt : híde not thy fáce from
me ; lést I be líke unto thém that go dówn *in*-to^
the pīt.

8 O lét me héar thy lóving-kíndness betímes
in the mórning ; for in *thée* is my trúst : shéw
thou me the wáy that I should wálk in ; for I líft
up my sóul *un*-to thëe.

9 Delíver me, O Lórd, *from* mine^é-ne-mies :
for I flée unto thée *to* híde më.

10 Téach me to do the thíng that pléaseth thee,
for *thóu* art my Gód : let thy lóving Spírit léad
me fórth into the länd *of* rígh꞊teous-nëss.

11 Quícken me, O *Lórd*, for^thy Náme's sáke :
and for thy ríghteousness' sáke bring my sóul
out *of* tróu-blë.

12 And of thy góodness *sláy* mine^é-ne-mies :
and destróy all thém that véx my sóul ; for I ám
thy sér-vänt.

Glóry be to the *Fá*-ther,^and^to the Són :
and to *the* Hó꞊ly Ghöst.

As it wás in the begínning, is nów, and *év*-er
sháll be : wórld withóut *énd*.   A-mën.

THE 30th EVENING

PSALM 147   *Laudate Dominum*   TONE I

O PRÁISE the Lórd, for it is a góod thíng
to síng práises únto *our* Gód : yéa, a jóyful
and pléasant thíng it ís *to* be thänk-ful.

2 The Lórd doth buíld up Jerú-*sa*-lem : and
gáther togéther the óut-*casts* of Ïs-raᵓel.

3 He héaleth thóse that are bróken *in* héart :
and gíveth médicine to *héal* their sïck-ness.

4 He télleth the númber of *the* stárs : and
cálleth them *áll* by theïr námes.

5 Gréat is our Lórd, and gréat is his *pów*-er :
yéa, and his wís-*dom* is ïn-fiᵓnite.

6 The Lórd setteth úp *the* méek : and bríngeth
the ungódly *dówn* to thë gróund.

7 O síng unto the Lórd with thánks-*giv*-ing :
sing práises upon the hárp *un*-to öur Gód ;

8 Who cóvereth the héaven with clóuds ; and
prepáreth raín for *the* éarth : and máketh the
gráss to grów upon the móuntains ; and hérb
for the üse ofˆmén ;

9 Who gíveth fódder unto the *cát*-tle : and
féedeth the young rávens that *cáll* up-ön him.

10 He hath nó pléasure in the stréngth of *an*
hórse : neíther delíghteth he in *a*-ny män's légs.

11 But the Lórd's delíght is in thém that *féar* him : and pút their trúst *in* his mër-cy.

12 Praíse the Lórd, O Jerú-*sa*-lem : praíse thy *Gód*, O Sÿ-on.

13 For he hath máde fást the bárs of *thy* gátes : and hath bléssed thy chíl-*dren* with-ĭn thee.

14 He máketh péace in thy *bór*-ders : and fílleth thee *with* the flöur of⌒whéat.

15 He séndeth fórth his commándment up-*on* eárth : and his wórd rúnneth *ve*-ry swíft-ly.

16 He gíveth snów *like* wóol : and scáttereth the hóar-*frost* like äsh-es.

17 He cásteth fórth his íce like *mór*-sels : who is áble *to* a-bĭde his⌒fróst ?

18 He séndeth out his wórd, and mélt-*eth* thém : he blóweth with his wínd, *and* the wä-ters⌒flów.

19 He shéweth his wórd unto *Já*-cob : his státutes and órdinances *un*-to Ĭs-ra-̂el.

20 He hath nót dealt só with ány *ná*-tion : neíther have the héathen *knów*-ledge öf his⌒láws.

Glóry be to the Fáther, and to *the* Són : and *to* the Hö-ly⌒Ghóst.

As it wás in the begínning, is nów, and éver *sháll* be : wórld with-*óut* énd.   Ä-men.

Psalm 148   *Laudate Dominum*   Tone VII

O PRÁISE the *Lórd* of héa-ven : *praise* him
in^the heíght.

2 Praíse him, áll ye *án*-gels of hís : *praise* him,
áll^his hóst.

3 *Praise* him, sún^and móon : praíse him, *áll*
ye stárs^and líght.

4 Praíse him, *áll* ye héa-vens : and ye wáters
that are a-*bóve* the héa-vens.

5 Let them praíse the *Náme* of the Lórd : for
he spáke the wórd, and théy were máde ; he
commánded, and théy *were* cre-á-ted.

6 He hath máde them fást for *év*-er^and év-er :
he hath gíven them a láw which shall *nót* be
bró-ken.

7 Praíse the *Lórd* up-on eárth : ye *drá*-gons,^
and áll déeps ;

8 Fíre and haíl, *snów* and vá-pours : wínd and
stórm, ful-*fíl*-ling his wórd ;

9 *Móun*-tains^and áll hílls : fruítful *trées* and^all
cé-dars ;

10 *Béasts* and^all cát-tle : wórms and *féa*-ther-ed
fówls ;

11 Kíngs of the *éarth* and^áll péo-ple : prínces
and áll *júdg*-es of^the wórld ;

12 Yóung men and maídens, óld men and

chíldren; praíse the *Náme* of the Lórd : for his
Náme ónly is excéllent; and his práise above
héa-ven and eárth.

13 He shall exált the hórn of his péople; áll his
saints shall praíse him : éven the chíldren of
'Israel; éven the *péo*-ple˄that sér˄veth him.

Glóry be to the *Fá*-ther,˄and to˄the Són : and
to the Hó˗ly Ghóst.

As it wás in the begínning, is nów, and *év-er*
sháll be : wórld with-*óut* énd.   A-men.

PSALM 149   *Cantate Domino*   TONE VI

O SÍNG unto the *Lórd* a néw sóng : let the
congregátion *of* saínts praíse him.

2 Let 'Israel rejoíce in *hím* that máde him :
and let the chíldren of Sýon be jóy-*ful* ïn theír
Kíng.

3 Let them praíse his *Náme* in the dánce :
let them síng praíses unto hím with *tá*-brët and
hárp.

4 For the Lórd hath pléasure *in* his péo-ple :
and hélpeth *the* mëek-heart-ed.

5 Let the saínts be *jóy*-ful˄with gló-ry : let
them re-*joíce* ïn theír béds.

6 Let the praíses of Gód *be* in theír móuth :
and a twó-édged *swórd* ïn theír hánds;

7 To be avénged *of* the héa-then : and to
re-*buke* thë peo-ple;

8 To *bind* their kíngs^in chaíns : and their
nóbles with *links* öf í-ron.

9 That théy may be avénged of them, *as* it^is
writ-ten : Such hó-*nour* häve áll his^saínts.

Glóry be to the *Fá*-ther,^and to^the Són :
and *to* thë Hó-ly^Ghóst.

As it wás in the begínning, is nów, and *év*-er
sháll be : wórld with-*óut* ënd.   A-men.

PSALM 150   *Laudate Dominum*   TONE VIII

O PRÁISE Gód in his *hó*-li^ness : praíse him
in the fírmament *of* his pów-er.

2 Praíse him in his nóble *ácts* : praíse him
accórding to his éx-*cel*-lent gréat-ness.

3 Praíse him in the sóund of the *trúm*-pet :
praíse him up-*ón* the lúte and^hárp.

4 Praíse him in the cýmbals and *dán*-ces : praíse
him up-*ón* the stríngs and^pípe.

5 Praíse him upon the wéll-túned *cým*-bals :
praíse him upón *the* lóud cým-bals.

6 Let évery thing that hath *bréath* : — praíse
the^Lórd.

Glóry be to the Fáther, and to the *Són* : and
to the Hó-ly^Ghóst.

As it wás in the begínning, is nów, and éver
sháll be : wórld with-*óut* énd.   A-men.

CHRISTMAS EVENING

PSALM 89   *Misericordias Domini*   TONE VIII

MY SONG shall be álway of the lóving-kíndness of the *Lórd* : with my móuth will I éver be shéwing thy trúth from óne generátion *to* a-nó⌢ther.

2 For I have saíd ; Mércy shall be set úp for *év*-er : thy trúth shalt thou stáblish *in* the héa⌢vens.

3 I have máde a cóvenant with my *chó*-sen : I have swórn unto Dá-*vid* my sér⌢vant ;

4 Thy séed will I stáblish for *év*-er : and sét up thy thróne from óne generátion *to* a-nó⌢ther.

5 O Lórd, the véry héavens shall praíse thy wóndrous *wórks* : and thy trúth in the cóngre-*gá*-tion of⌢the⌢saínts.

6 For whó is hé amóng the *clóuds* : that shall be compár-*ed* un-to⌢the⌢Lórd ?

7 And whát is hé amóng the *góds* : that shall be *líke* un-to⌢the⌢Lórd ?

8 Gód is véry gréatly to be féared in the cóuncil of the *saínts* : and to be hád in réverence of áll thém that are *róund* a-bóut⌢him.

9 O Lórd Gód of hósts, whó is líke unto *thée* : thy trúth, most míghty Lórd, *is* on év⌢ery⌢síde.

10 Thou rúlest the ráging of the *séa* : thou stíllest the wáves there-*óf* when théy^a^ríse.

11 Thou hast subdúed 'Egypt, and de-*stróy*-ed^it : thou hast scáttered thine énemies abróad *with* thy mígh^ty^árm.

12 The héavens are thíne ; the éarth álso is *thíne* : thou hast laíd the foundátion of the róund wórld, and *áll* that thére^in^is.

13 Thou hast máde the nórth and the *sóuth* : Tábor and Hérmon shall re-*jóice* in thý^Náme.

14 Thou hást a míghty *árm* : stróng is thy hánd, and hígh *is* thy ríght^hánd.

15 Ríghteousness and équity are the habitátion of thy *séat* : mércy and trúth shall *gó* be-fóre^thy^ fáce.

16 Bléssed is the péople, O Lórd, that can rejoíce in *thée* : they shall wálk in the líght *of* thy cóun^te^nance.

17 Their delíght shall be daíly in thy *Náme* : and in thy ríghteousness *shall* they máke^their^ bóast.

18 For thóu art the glóry of their *stréngth* : and in thy lóving-kíndness thou *shalt* líft up^our^ hórns.

19 For the Lórd is óur de-*fénce* : the Hóly One of 'Isra-*el* is óur^Kíng.

20 Thou spákest sómetime in vísions unto thy saínts, and *saídst* : I have laíd hélp upon óne that is míghty ; I have exálted one chósen óut *of* the péo^ple.

21 I have fóund Dávid my *sér*-vant : with my hóly oíl have *I* a-noín⌣ted^him.

22 My hánd shall hóld him *fást* : and my *árm* shall stréng⌣then^him.

23 The énemy shall nót be áble to dó him *ví*-o⌣lence : the són of wíckedness *sháll* not húrt^him.

24 I will smíte dówn his fóes befóre his *fáce* : and plágue *thém* that háte^him.

25 My trúth álso and my mércy shall be *wíth* him : and in my Náme shall his hórn *bé* ex-ált⌣ed.

26 I will sét his domínion álso in the *séa* : and his *ríght* hánd in^the^flóods.

27 He shall cáll me ; Thóu art my *Fá*-ther : my Gód, and my *stróng* sal-vá⌣tion.

28 And I will máke him my *fírst*-born : hígher than the kíngs *of* the eárth.

29 My mércy will I kéep for hím for éver-*móre* : and my cóvenant shall stánd *fást* with him.

30 His séed also will I máke to endúre for *év*-er : and his thróne as the *dáys* of héa⌣ven.

31 But if his chíldren forsáke my *láw* : and wálk not *ín* my júdge⌣ments ;

32 If they bréak my státutes, and kéep not mý com-*mánd*-ments : I will vísit their offénces with the ród ; and their *sín* with scóurg⌣es.

33 Névertheless, my lóving-kíndness will I not útterly táke from *hím* : nor súf-*fer* my trúth^to^faíl.

34 My cóvenant will I not bréak; nor álter the
thíng that is gone óut of my *lĭps* : I have swórn
ónce by my hóliness, that I will *nŏt* fail Dá͜vid.

35 His séed shall endúre for *ĕv*-er : and his séat
is líke as the *sŭn* be-fóre^me.

36 He shall stánd fást for évermore as the *mŏon* :
and as the faíthful wít-*ness* in héa͜ven.

37 But thóu hast abhórred and fórsaken thine
A-*nŏĭn*-ted : and art dis-*pléas*-ed at^him.

38 Thóu hast bróken the cóvenant of thy *sĕr*-vant :
and cást his crówn *to* the gróund.

39 Thóu hast óverthrown áll his *hĕdg*-es : and
bróken *dŏwn* his stróng^holds.

40 All théy that go bý *spŏĭl* him : and he is
becóme a repróach *tŏ* his neígh͜bours.

41 Thóu hast sét up the ríght hánd of his
ĕn-e͜mies : and made áll his ádver-*sa*-ries to^
re͜joíce.

42 Thou hast táken awáy the édge of his *sword* :
and gívest him not víctory *in* the bát͜tle.

43 Thóu hast put óut his *glŏ*-ry : and cást his
thróne dówn *to* the gróund.

44 The dáys of his yóuth hast thou *shŏrt*-en͜ed :
and covered him *with* dis-hó͜nour.

45 Lórd, how lóng wilt thou híde thysélf, for
ĕv-er : and sháll *thy* wráth búrn^like^fíre ?

46 O remémber how shórt my *tĭme* is : whérefore hast thou *máde* áll mén^for^nóught ?

47 What mán is hé that líveth, and shall nót see

déath : and sháll he delíver his sóul *fróm* the
hánd⌒of⌒héll ?

48 Lórd, whére are thy óld lóving-*kínd*-ness⌐es :
which thou swárest unto Dá-*vid* in thý⌒trúth ?

49 Remémber, Lórd, the rebúke that thy sérvants
háve : and hów I do béar in my bósom the rebúkes
of *má*-ny péo⌐ple ;

50 Whérewith thine énemies have blasphémed
thee ; and slándered the fóotsteps of thíne
A-*nóin*-ted : Praísed be the Lórd for évermore.
A-*mén*, and A⌐men.

Glóry be to the Fáther, and to the *Són* : and
to the Hó⌐ly⌒Ghóst.

As it wás in the begínning, is nów, and éver
sháll be : wórld with-*óut* énd.   A⌐men.

PSALM. 110   *Dixit Dominus*   TONE VII

T HE LÓRD said *ún*-to my Lórd : Sít thou
on my ríght hánd ; untíl I máke thine
éne-*mies* thy föot-stool.

2 The Lórd shall sénd the ród of thy pówer
out of Sý-on : bé thou rúler ; éven in the mídst
a-*móng* thine ën-e⌐mies.

3 In the dáy of thy pówer shall the péople
óffer thee frée-will ófferings with an *hó*-ly wór-ship :
the déw of thy bírth is of the *wómb* of⌒the
mörn-ing.

4 The Lórd swáre, and *will* nót re-pént : Thóu
art a Príest for éver after the órder *of* Mel-
chĭ-se^dech.

5 The Lórd up-*ón* thy ríght hánd : shall wóund
even kíngs in the *dáy* of hīs wráth.

6 He shall júdge among the héathen ; he
shall fíll the pláces *with* the^déad bód-ies :
and smíte in sun⸱ler the héads over *dí*-vers
coün-tries.

7 He shall drínk of the *bróok* in the wáy : thérefore shall he *líft* up hīs héad.

Glóry be to the *Fá*-ther,^and to^the Són : and
to the Hö-ly^Ghóst.

As it wás in the begínning, is nów, and *év*-er
sháll be : wórld with-*óut* énd.   Ä-men.

PSALM 132   *Memento Domine*   TONE I

LÓRD, RE-mémber *Dá*-vid : and *áll* his
   tróu-blë ;

2 Hów he swáre únto *the* Lórd : and vówed a
vów unto the Almíghty G*ód* of Já-cöb ;

3 I will nót cóme within the tábernacle of
mine hóuse : nor clímb up *ín*-to my bëd ;

4 I will nót súffer mine éyes to sléep ; nor mine
éye-lids to *slúm*-ber : neíther the témples of my
héad *to* take á^ny rëst ;

5 Until I fínd out a pláce for the témple of *the* Lórd : an hábitation for the míghty *Gód* of Ja-cöb.

6 Ló, we héard of the sáme at 'E-*phra*-ta : and *foúnd* it in^the wöod.

7 We will gó into his táber-*na*-cle : and fáll lów on our knées be-*fóre* his fóot-stöol.

8 Aríse, O Lórd, into thy rést-*ing*-pláce : thóu, and the *árk* of thy strëngth.

9 Lét thy príests be clóthed with rígh-*teous*-ness : and lét thy saínts *síng* with jóy^ful-nëss.

10 For thy sérvant Dá-*vid's* sake : túrn not awáy the présence of *thíne* A-noín-tëd.

11 The Lórd hath máde a faíthful óath unto *Dá*-vid : and he *sháll* not shrínk^from ït ;

12 Of the fruít of thy *bó*-dy : shall I *sét* up-ón^ thy sëat.

13 If thy chíldren will kéep my cóvenant ; and my téstimonies that I shall *leárn* them : their chíldren also shall sít upon thy *séat* for év^er- -möre.

14 For the Lórd hath chósen Sýon to be an habitátion for *him*-sélf : he hath *lóng*-ed for hër.

15 Thís shall be my rést for *év*-er : hére will I dwéll, for I háve *a* de-líght^there-ïn.

16 I will bléss her víctuals with *ín*-crease : and will sátis-*fy* her póor^with brëad.

17 I will déck her príests *with* héalth : and her saínts *shall* re-joíce^and sïng.

18 Thére shall I máke the hórn of Dávid to

flóu-rish : I have ordaíned a lántern for *mine*
A-noin-tëd.

19 'As for his énemies, I shall clóthe them *with*
sháme : but upon himsélf shall *his* crówn flóu-rïsh.

Glóry be to the Fáther, and to *the* Són : and
to the Hó:ly Ghöst.

As it wás in the begínning, is nów, and éver
shall be : wórld with-*óut* énd.   A-mën.

ASH-WEDNESDAY EVENING

PSALM 102   *Domine exaudi*   TONE I

HEAR MY práyer, O Lórd : and let my
crýing *come* un-to thëe.

2 Híde not thy fáce from mé in the tíme of
my *tróu*-ble : inclíne thine éar unto mé when I
cáll ; O héar me, *and* that ríght söon.

3 For my dáys are consúmed awáy *like* smóke :
and my bónes are búrnt úp as it *wére* a fíre-
bränd.

4 My héart is smítten dówn, and wíthered *like*
gráss : so that I for-*get* to éat^my brëad.

5 For the voíce of my *gróan*-ing : my bónes will
scárce *cléave* to my flësh.

6 I am becóme like a pélican in the wíl-*der*-ness :
and like an ówl that is *in* the dé-sërt.

7 I have wátched, and am éven as it wére a *spár*-row : that sítteth alóne up-*ón* the hóuse-töp.

8 Mine énemies revíle me áll the *dáy* lóng : and théy that are mád upon me are swórn togé-*ther* a-gaínst më.

9 For I have éaten áshes as it *were* bréad : and míngled my *drínk* with wéep-ïng ;

10 And thát becáuse of thine indignátion *and* wráth : for thou hast táken me *úp,* and cástˆme döwn.

11 My dáys are góne like a *shá*-dow : and I am wí-*ther*-ed líke gräss.

12 But, thóu, O Lórd, shalt endúre for *év*-er : and thy remémbrance throughóut all *ge*-ne-rá-tïons.

13 Thóu shalt aríse, and have mércy upon *Sý*-on : for it is tíme that thóu have mércy upon her ; *yéa,* the tímeˆis cöme.

14 And whý ? thy sérvants thínk upon *her* stónes : and it pítieth them to *sée* her inˆthe düst.

15 The héathen shall féar thy Náme, O Lórd : and áll the kíngs of the *eárth* thy Máˀjes-tÿ ;

16 When the Lórd shall buíld up *Sý*-on : and whén his *gló*-ry shállˆap-pëar ;

17 When he túrneth him unto the práyer of the póor dé-*sti*-tute : and despí-*seth* not theírˆ de-sïre.

18 Thís shall be wrítten for thóse that come *áf*-ter : and the péople which shall be *boŕn* shall praíseˆthe Lörd.

I

19 For he hath lóoked dówn from his sánctu-*a*-ry :
out of the héaven did the *Lórd* be-hóld⌢the
ëarth ;

20 That he might héar the móurnings of súch
as are ín captí-*vi*-ty : and delíver the chíldren
ap-*póint*-ed un⌢to dëath ;

21 That théy may decláre the Náme of the Lórd
in *Sý*-on : and his wórship *at* Je-rú⌢sa-lëm ;

22 When the péople are gáthered to-*gé*-ther :
and the kíngdoms ál-*so*, to sérve⌢the Lörd.

23 He bróught dówn my stréngth in my *jóur*-ney :
and shórt-*en*-ed my däys.

24 But I saíd ; 'O my Gód, táke me not awáy
in the mídst of *mine* áge : as for thý yeárs, they
endúre throughóut all *gé*-ne-rá-tïons.

25 Thóu, Lórd, in the begínning hast laíd the
foundátion of *the* eárth : and the héavens are the
wórk of thy händs.

26 Théy shall pérish, but thóu shalt *en*-dúre :
they áll shall wáx óld as *dóth* a gár-mënt ;

27 And as a vésture shalt thou chánge them, and
théy shall be *chán*-ged : but thóu art the sáme,
and thy *yéars* shall nót faïl.

28 The chíldren of thy sérvants shall con-*tín*-ue :
and their séed shall stánd *fást* in thy sïght.

Glóry be to the Fáther, and to *the* Són : and
to the Hó⌢ly Ghöst.

As it wás in the begínning, is nów, and éver
sháll be : wórld with-*óut* énd.   A-mën.

PSALM 130 *De profundis* TONE VIII

OUT OF the déep have I cálled unto thée,
O *Lórd* : Lórd, *héar* my⌃voíce.

2 O lét thine éars consíder *wéll* : the voíce of
my com⌐plaínt.

3 If thóu, Lórd, wilt be extréme to márk what
is dóne a-*miss* : O Lórd, whó may a-*bíde* it?

4 For there is mércy with *thée* : thérefore shalt
thóu be *féar*-ed.

5 I lóok for the Lórd; my sóul doth wáit for
him : in his wórd is *my* trúst.

6 My sóul fléeth únto the *Lórd* : befóre the
mórning wátch, I sáy, befóre the *mórn*-ing⌃
wátch.

7 O 'Israel, trúst in the Lórd; for with the
Lórd there is *mér*-cy : and with hím is plénteous
re-*démp*-tion.

8 And hé shall redéem '*Is*-ra⌐el : from *áll*
his⌃síns.

Glóry be to the Fáther, and to the *Són* : and
to the *Hó*-ly⌃Ghóst.

As it wás in the begínning, is nów, and éver
sháll be : wórld withóut énd.   *A*-men.

PSALM 143   *Domine exaudi*   TONE IV

HEAR MY práyer, O Lórd, and consíder *my* de-síre : héarken unto mé for thy trúth *and* rígh-teous-ness säke.

2 And énter not into júdgement *with* thy sér-vant : for in thy síght shall nó man líving *be* jús-ti-fi-ëd.

3 For the énemy hath pérsecuted my sóul ; he hath smítten my lífe dówn *to* the gróund : he hath laíd me in the dárkness ; as the mén *that* have been lóng dëad.

4 Thérefore is my spírit véx-*ed* with-ín me : and my héart with-*in* me is dé⌒so-läte.

5 Yét do I remémber the tíme pást ; I múse upon *áll* thy wórks : yéa, I éxercise mysélf in *the* wórks of thy händs.

6 I strétch fórth my hánds *un*-to thée : my sóul gáspeth unto *thée* as a thír⌒sty länd.

7 Héar me, O Lórd, and thát sóon ; for my spírit *wáx*-eth faínt : híde not thy fáce from mé ; lést I be líke unto thém that *go* dówn in-to⌒the pït.

8 O lét me héar thy lóving-kíndness betímes in the mórning ; for in thée *is* my trúst : shéw thou mé the wáy that 'I should wálk in ; for I líft up *my* sóul un-to thëe.

9 Delíver me, O Lórd, *from* mine én-e⌒mies :
for I flée un-*to* thée to híde më.

10 Téach me to dó the thíng that pléaseth thee,
for thóu *art* my Gód : let thy lóving Spírit léad
me fórth into *the* land of rígh⌒teous-nëss.

11 Quícken me, O Lórd, *for* thy Náme's sáke :
and for thy ríghteousness' sáke bring my *sóul*
out of tróu-blë.

12 And of thy goódness *sláy* mine én-e⌒mies :
and destróy all thém that véx my sóul ; for '*I*
am thy sér-vänt.

Glóry be to the Fáther, and to the *Són* : *and*
to the Hó⌒ly Ghöst.

As it wás in the begínning, is nów, and *év*-er
sháll be : wórld *with*-óut énd.   A-mën.

GOOD FRIDAY EVENING

<small>Psalm</small> 69   *Salvum me fac*   <small>Tonus in Directum</small>

Sáve *me*, O Gód : for the wáters are c⌒ome
ín, éven únto *my* sóul.

2 I stíck fást in the deep míre, *where* no gróund⌒
is : I am cóme into déep wáters, so that the flóods
run ó-*ver* me.

3 I am wéary of crýing ; my *thróat* is drý : my
síght faíleth me for waíting so l⌒ng upon *my*
Gód.

4 Théy that háte me withóut a caúse are móre than the haírs *of* my héad : théy that áre mine énemies, and would destróy me guíltless, are mígh-*ty.*

5 I paíd them the thíngs that I *né*-ver tóok : Gód, thou knówest my símpleness, and my faúlts are not híd *from* thee.

6 Lét not thém that trúst in thée, O Lórd Gód of hósts, be ashámed *for* my caúse : lét not thóse that séek thee be confóunded through mé ; O Lórd Gód of 'Is-*ra*˷el.

7 And whý? for thy sáke have I súffer-*ed* re-próof : sháme hath cóvered *my* fáce.

8 I am becóme a stránger un-*to* my bré˷thren : éven an álien unto my móther's chíl-*dren.*

9 For the zéal of thine hóuse hath éven *éat*-en me : and the rebúkes of thém that rebúked thee are fállen up-*ón* me.

10 I wépt, and chástened my-*sélf* with fást˷ing : and thát was túrned to mý *re*-próof.

11 I pút on *sáck*-cloth ál˷so : and they jésted up-*ón* me.

12 Théy that sít in the gáte *spéak* a-gaínst^me : and the drúnkards make sóngs up-*ón* me.

13 But, Lórd, I máke my práyer *un*-to thée : in an accépta-*ble* tíme.

14 Héar me, O Gód, in the múltitude *of* thy mér˷cy : even in the trúth of thý salvá-*tion.*

15 Táke me óut of the míre, *that* I sínk^not :

O lét me be delívered from thém that háte me;
and óut of the déep wá-*ters*.

16 Lét not the wáter-flóod drówn me; neíther
let the déep swál-*low* me úp : and lét not the
pít shut her móuth up-*ón* me.

17 Héar me, O Lórd, for thy lóving-kíndness
is *cóm*-fort-a⌒ble : túrn thee únto me accórding
to the múltitude of thy mér-*cies*.

18 And híde not thy fáce from thy sérvant, for
'I *am* in tróu⌒ble : O háste thee, and *héar* me.

19 Dráw nígh unto my *sóul*, and sáve⌒it : O
delíver me, becaúse of mine én-*e*⌒mies.

20 Thóu hast knówn my repróof, my sháme, and
my dis-hón⌒our : mine ádversaries are áll in *thy*
síght.

21 Thy rebúke hath bróken my héart; I am
fúll of héa⌒vi⌒ness : I lóoked for sóme to have
píty on me, but thére was nó man; neíther fóund
I ány to cóm-*fort* me.

22 They gáve me *gáll* to éat : and whén I was
thírsty they gáve me vinegar *to* drínk.

23 Lét their táble be máde a snáre to táke
them-*selves* with-ál : and lét the thíngs that
shóuld have béen for their wéalth be unto thém
an occásion of fáll-*ing*.

24 Let their éyes be blínded, *that* they sée⌒
not : and éver bów thou dówn *their* bácks.

25 Póur out thine indigná-*tion* up-ón⌒them : and
lét thy wráthful displéasure take hóld *of* them.

26 Lét their hábitá-*tion* be vóid : and nó man to dwéll in *their* ténts.

27 For they pérsecute hím whom *thóu* hast smít⌐ten : and they tálk hów they may véx thém whom thóu hast wóund-*ed*.

28 Lét them fáll from óne wíckedness *to* an-ó⌐ther : and nót come ínto thy rígh-*teous*⌐ness.

29 Lét them be wíped óut of the bóok *of* the lív-ing : and nót be wrítten amóng the rígh-*teous*.

30 'As for mé, when I am póor *and* in héa⌐ví⌐ness : thy hélp, O Gód, shall líft *me* úp.

31 I will práise the Náme of Gód *with* a sóng : and mágnify it with thanksgív-*ing*.

32 This álso shall *pléase* the Lórd : bétter than a búllock that hath hórns *and* hóofs.

33 The húmble shall consíder this, *and* be glád : séek ye áfter Gód, and your sóul *shall* líve.

34 For the Lórd héar-*eth* the póor : and despíseth not his prí-*son*⌐ers.ꞌ

35 Let héaven *and* éarth práise⌐him : the séa, and áll that móveth *there*-ín.

36 For Gód will sáve Sýon, and búild the cí-*ties* of Jú⌐dah : that mén may dwéll thére, and háve it in possés-*sion*.

37 The postérity álso of his servánts shall in-*hé*-rit it : and théy that lóve his Náme shall dwéll *there*-ín.

Glóry be to the Fáther, and *to* the Són : and to the Hó-*ly* Ghóst.

As it wás in the begínning, is nów, and *év-*er shálĺ⌐be : wórld with-óut énd. *A*-men.

PSALM 88 *Domine Deus* TONUS IN DIRECTUM

O LORD Gód of my salvation, I have críed dáy and níght *be*^fóre thee : O lét my práyer énter into thy présence ; inclíne thine éar un-*to* my cáll-ing.

2 For my sóul is fúll *of*^tróu-ble : and my lífe draweth *nigh* un-to héll.

3 I am cóunted as óne of thém that go dówn *in*^to the^gráve : and I have been éven as a mán *that* hath nó stréngth.

4 Frée among the déad ; líke unto thém that are wóunded, and *lie*^in the^gráve : who are óut of remémbrance ; and are cút a-*way* from thy hánd.

5 Thou hast láid me in *the*^lów-est^pít : in a pláce of dárk-*ness*, and in the^déep.

6 Thine índignátion lieth hárd *up*^ón mé : and thou hast véxed *me* with áll thy^stórms.

7 Thou hast pút awáy mine acquaín-*tance*^fár from^mé : and máde me to be ab-*hor*-red of thém.

8 I am so fást *in*^prí-son : that I *cán*-not get fórth.

9 My síght faíleth me for vé-*ry*^tróu-ble : Lórd, I have cálled dáily upón thee ; I have strétched forth my *hands* un-to thée.

10 Dóst thou shew wónders a͡-móng the^déad :
or shǎll the déad ríse up a-*gáin*, and praíse thee ?

11 Shǎll thy lóving-kíndness be shéw-*ed*^in the^
gráve : or thy faíthfulness *in* de-strúc-tion ?

12 Shǎll thy wóndrous wórks be knówn *in*^the
dárk : and thy ríghteousness in the lánd where
ǎll things *are* for-gót-ten ?

13 Unto thée have I crí-*ed*,^O Lórd : and éarly
shall my práyer *come* be-fóre thee.

14 Lórd, why abhór-*rest*^thou my^sóul : and
hídest *thou* thy fáce from^me ?

15 I am in mísery, and líke unto hím that is at
the^poínt to^díe : éven from my yóuth úp, thy
térrors have I súffered *with* a tróu-bled^mínd.

16 Thy wráthful displéasure gó-*eth*^ó-ver^me :
and the féar of thée *hath* un-dóne me.

17 They cáme about me daíly *like*^wá-ter : and
cómpassed me togé-*ther* on év-ery^síde.

18 My lóvers and fríends hast thou pút a͡-wáy
from^me : and híd mine acquaíntance *óut* of my
síght.

Glóry be to the Fáther, *and*^to the^Són : and
to·the Hó-ly^Ghóst.

As it wás in the begínning, is nów, and év-*er*^
shǎll be : wórld with-*óut* énd.   A-men.

EASTER EVENING

PRÁISE THE Lórd, ye *sér*-vants : O praíse the *Náme* of the Lórd.

2 Bléssed be the Náme of the *Lórd* : from thís time *fórth* for év-er⌒more.

3 The Lórd's Náme is *praí*-sed : from the rísing up of the sún unto the góing *dówn* of the sáme.

4 The Lórd is hígh above all *héa*-then : and his glóry a-*bóve* the héa-vens.

5 Whó is líke unto the Lórd our Gód; that háth his dwélling so *hígh* : and yet húmbleth himsélf to behóld the thíngs that are in *héa*-ven and eárth ?

6 He táketh up the símple óut of the *dúst* : and lífteth the póor *óut* of the míre ;

7 That he may sét him with the *prín*-ces : éven with the prínces *of* his péo-ple.

8 He máketh the bárren wóman to kéep *hóuse* : and to be a jóyful mó-*ther* of chíl-dren.

Glóry be to the Fáther, and to the *Són* : and *to* the Hó-ly⌒Ghóst.

As it wás in the begínning, is nów, and éver *shall* be : wórld with-*óut* énd. A-men.

PSALM 114　　*In exitu Israel*　　PEREGRINE TONE

WHEN 'Israel came *óut* of 'E-gypt : ÄND the hóuse of Jácob from amóng the *stránge* péo-plë,

2 Júdah was his *sánc*-tu-a-ry : and 'Israel his *do*-mín-īon.

3 The séa *saw* thát, and fléd : Jórdan *was* drí⌐ven bäck.

4 The móuntains *skip*-ped like ráms : and the líttle hílls *like* yóung shëep.

5 What aíleth thee, O thou séa, *that* thou fléd-dest : and thou Jórdan, that thóu *wast* drí⌐ven bäck ?

6 Ye móuntains, that ye *skip*-ped like ráms : and ye líttle hílls, *like* yóung shëep ?

7 Trémble, thou éarth, at the *pré*-sence of the⌐ Lórd : at the présence of the Gód *of* Já-cöb ;

8 Who túrned the hárd róck into a *stánd*-ing ẃater : and the flínt-stone ínto *a* spríng⌐ing wëll.

Glóry be to the Fá-*ther*, and to the⌐Són : and to *the* Hó⌐ly Ghöst.

.As it wás in the begínning, is nów, and *év*-er sháll be : wórld withóut *énd*.　A-mën.

PSALM 118   *Confitemini Domino*   TONE VIII

O GIVE thánks unto the Lórd, for he is *grá*-cious : because his mércy endúr-*eth* for év-er.

2 Let 'Israel now cónfess, that he is *grá*-cious : and that his mércy endúr-*eth* for év-er.

3 Let the hóuse of 'Aaron nów con-*féss* : that his mércy endúr-*eth* for év-er.

4 Yéa, let them nów that féar the Lórd con-*féss* : that his mércy endúr-*eth* for év-er.

5 I cálled upon the Lórd in *tróu*-ble : and the Lórd *héard* me at lárge.

6 The Lórd is on my *síde* : I will not féar what mán *do*-eth ún-to^me.

7 The Lórd táketh my párt with thém that *hélp* me : thérefore shall I sée my desíre up-*on* mine én-e^mies.

8 It is bétter to trúst in the *Lórd* : than to put any cón-*fi*-dence in mán.

9 It is bétter to trúst in the *Lórd* : than to put any cónfi-*dence* in prín-ces.

10 'All nátions cómpassed me róund a-*bóut* : but in the Náme of the Lórd will *I* de-stróy them.

11 They képt me ín on évery síde ; they képt me ín, I śay, on évery *síde* : but in the Náme of the Lórd will *I* de-stróy them.

12 They cáme abóut me like bées; and are extínct éven as the fíre amóng the *thórns* : for in the Náme of the Lórd I *will* de-stróy them.

13 Thou hast thrúst sóre at me, that I might *fáll* : but the *Lórd* was my hélp.

14 The Lórd is my stréngth, and my *sóng* : and is becóme *my* sal-vá-tion.

15 The voíce of jóy and héalth is in the dwéllings of the *rígh*-teous : the ríght hánd of the Lórd bríngeth *mígh*-ty thíngs to^páss.

16 The ríght hánd of the Lórd hath the pre-*é*-mi^nence : the ríght hánd of the Lórd bringeth *mígh*-ty thíngs to^páss.

17 I shóll not díe, but *líve* : and declóre the *wórks* of the Lórd.

18 The Lórd hath chástened and cor-*réct*-ed^me : but he háth not gíven me ó-ver un-to^déath.

19 'Ópen me the gátes of *rígh*-teous^ness : that I may go ínto them, and give *thánks* un-to the^ Lórd.

20 Thís is the gáte of the *Lórd* : the ríghteous shall *én*-ter in-to^it.

21 I will thánk thee, for thóu hast *héard* me : and art becóme *my* sal-vá-tion.

22 The sáme stóne which the búilders re-*fú*-sed : is becóme the héad-stone *in* the córner.

23 Thís is the Lórd's *dó*-ing : and it is márvel-*lous* in our éyes.

24 Thís is the dáy which the Lórd hath *máde* : wé will rejoice *and* be glád in^it.

25 Hélp me nów, O *Lórd* : O Lórd, send us *nów* pros-pé-ri⌐ty.

26 Bléssed be hé that cómeth in the Náme of the *Lórd* : we have wíshed you good lúck ; yé that are of the *hóuse* of the Lórd.

27 Gód is the Lórd who hath shéwed us *light* : bínd the sácrifice with córds ; yéa, éven unto the hórns *of* the ál-tar.

28 Thóu art my Gód, and I will *thánk* thee : 'thou art my 'God, and *I* will praíse thee.

29 O give thánks unto the Lórd, for he is *grá*-cious : and his mércy endúr-*eth* for év-er.

Glóry be to the Fáther, and to the *Són* : and *to* the Hó-ly⌐Ghóst.

As it wás in the begínning, is nów, and éver *shall* be : wórld with-*óut* énd.   A-men.

ASCENSION   EVENING

Psalm 24   *Domini est terra*   Tone I

THE EÁRTH is the Lórd's, and áll that thére-*in* ís : the cómpass of the wórld, and *théy* that dwéll there⌐in.

2 For hé hath fóunded it upón *the* séas : and prepáred *it* up-ön the⌐flóods.

3 Whó shall ascénd into the híll of *the* Lórd : or whó shall ríse úp *in* his hö-ly⌐pláce ?

4 'Even hé that hath cléan hands, and a *púre*
héart : and háth not líft up his mínd unto vánity ;
nor swórn to de-*ceíve* his neīgh-bour.

5 Hé shall receíve the bléssing from *the* Lórd :
and ríghteousness from the Gód of *his* sal-vä-tion.

6 Thís is the generátion of thém that *séek* him :
éven of thém that séek thy *fáce*, O Jä-cob.

7 Líft up your héads, O ye gátes ; and bé ye
lift úp, ye éverlast-*ing* dóors : and the Kíng of
gló-*ry* shall cöme in.

8 Whó is the Kíng of *gló*-ry : it is the Lórd
stróng and míghty ; éven the Lórd mígh-*ty* in
bät-tle.

9 Líft up your héads, O ye gátes ; and bé ye
lift úp, ye éverlast-*ing* dóors : and the Kíng of
gló-*ry* shall cöme in.

10 Whó is the Kíng of *gló*-ry : éven the Lórd
of hósts, hé is the *Kíng* of glö-ry.

    Glóry be to the Fáther, and to *the* Són : and
to the Hö-ly^Ghóst.

    As it wás in the begínning, is nów, and éver
sháll be : wórld with-*óut* énd.   Ä-men.

PSALM 47   *Omnes gentes plaudite*   TONE VII

O CLÁP your hánds togéther, *áll* ye péople :
    O síng unto Gód with the *voíce* of mé-lo-dy.

2 For the Lórd is hígh, and *to* be féar-ed : he ís the gréat *Kíng* up⌐on áll⌐the éarth.

3 He shall subdúe the *péo*-ple ún⌐der us : and the nátions *uń*-der our féet.

4 He shall choose óut an *hé*-ri⌐tage for ús : éven the wórship of Jácob, *whóm* he lóv-ed.

5 Gód is gone úp *with* a mér⌐ry noíse : and the Lórd with the *soúnd* of the trúmp.

6 O síng praíses ; síng praíses *ún*-to our Gód : O síng praíses ; síng práises *ún*-to our Kíng.

7 For Gód is the *Kíng* of all⌐the éarth : síng ye praíses with *ún*-der-stánd-ing.

8 Gód reígneth *ó*-ver⌐the héa-then : Gód sítteth up-*ón* his hó⌐ly séat.

9 The prínces of the péople are joíned unto the péople of the *Gód* of 'A⌐bra-ham : for Gód, which is véry hígh exálted ; doth defénd the éarth, as it *wére* with a shíeld.

Glóry be to the *Fá*-ther,⌐and to⌐the Són : and *to* the Hó⌐ly Ghóst.

As it wás in the begínning, is nów, and *év*-er sháll be : wórld with-*óut* énd. A-men.

PSALM 108   *Paratum cor meum*   TONE VIII

O GÓD, my héart is réady, my héart is *réa*-dy : I will síng and give praíse with the best mém-*ber* that I have.

2 Awáke, thou lúte, and *hárp* : I mysélf will
a-*wáke* right éar-ly.

3 I will give thanks unto thée, O Lórd, amóng
the *péo*-ple : I will sing praíses unto thée a-*móng*
the ná-tions.

4 For thy mércy is gréater than the *héa*-vens :
and thy trúth réach-*eth* un-to the⌢clóuds.

5 Sét up thysélf, O Gód, abóve the *héa*-vens :
and thy glóry *a*-bóve áll the⌢eárth.

6 That thy belóved may be de-*li*-ver⌢ed : let
thy ríght hánd sáve *them*, and héar thou⌢me.

7 Gód hath spóken in his *hó*-li⌢ness : I will
rejoíce thérefore, and divíde Sýchem ; and mete
óut the vál-*ley* of Súc-coth.

8 Gílead is míne, and Manásses is *mine* : 'E-
phraim álso is the *stréngth* of my héad.

9 Júdah is my láw-giver, Móab is my *wásh*-pot :
over 'Edom will I cást out my shóe ; .upon
Philístia *will* I trí-umph.

10 Whó will léad me into the stróng *cí*-ty : and
whó will bríng me *in*-to 'E-dom ?

11 Hást not thóu forsáken us, O *Gód* : and wílt
not thóu, O Gód, go *fórth* with our hósts ?

12 O hélp us agaínst the *én*-e⌢my : for vaín *is*
the hélp of⌢mán.

13 Through Gód we shall dó great *ácts* : and it is
hé that shall tréad *dówn* our én-e⌢mies.

Glóry be to the Fáther, and to the *Són* : and
to the Hó-ly⌢Ghóst.

As it wás in the begínning, is nów, and éver
sháll be : wórld with-*óut* end.   A-men.

WHITSUN-DAY EVENING

PSALM 104   *Benedic anima mea*   TONE I

PRÁISE THE Lórd, O *my* sóul : O Lórd my Gód, thou art becóme exceéding glórious ; thou art clóthed with májes-*ty* and hö-nour.

2 Thou déckest thysélf with líght as it wére with a *gár*-ment : and spréadest out the héavens *like* a cür-tain.

3 Who láyeth the béams of his chámbers in the *wá*-ters : and máketh the clóuds his cháriot, and wálketh upón the *wings* of thë wínd.

4 He máketh his ángels *spi*-rits : and his mínis-*ters* a fläm-ing^fíre.

5 He laíd the foundátions of *the* eárth : that it néver should *móve* at ä-ny^tíme.

6 Thou cóveredst it with the déep líke as with a *gár*-ment : the wáters *stánd* in thë hílls.

7 At thý rebúke *they* flée : at the voíce of thy thún-*der* they äre a⌐fraíd.

8 They go úp as hígh as the hílls ; and dówn to the válleys *be*-néath : éven unto the pláce which thou hast ap-*póint*-ed för them.

9 Thou hast sét them their bóunds which they sháll *not* páss : néither túrn agaín to *cóv*-er thë éarth.

10 He séndeth the spríngs into the *rí*-vers : which *rún* a-möng the^hílls.

11 All béasts of the fíeld drínk *there*-óf : and the wíld *áss*-es quënch their^thírst.

12 Besíde them shall the fówls of the aír have their hábi-*ta*-tion : and síng a-*moṅg* the brän-ches.

13 He wátereth the hílls from *a*-bové : the eárth is fílled with the *frúit* of thÿ wórks.

14 He bríngeth forth gráss for the *cát*-tle : and gréen hérb for the *sér*-vice öf mén ;

15 That he may bring fóod out of the eárth; and wíne that maketh glád the héart *of* mán : and oíl to máke him a chéerful cóuntenance ; and bréad to *streṅgth*-en män's héart.

16 The trées of the Lórd álso are fúll *of* sáp : éven the cédars of Líbanus which *he* hath plän-ted ;

17 Whérein the bírds máke *their* nésts : and the fír-trees are a *dwéll*-ing för the^stórk.

18 The hígh hílls are a refúge for the *wíld* góats : and só are the stóny rócks *for* the cö-nies.

19 He appoínted the móon for cértain *séa*-sons : and the sún knów-*eth* his gö-ing^dówn.

20 Thou mákest dárkness that it máy *be* níght : wherein áll the béasts of the *fór*-est dö móve.

21 The líons róaring áfter *their* préy : do *séek* their mëat from^Gód.

22 The sún aríseth, and they gét them awáy to-*gé*-ther : and láy them *dówn* in theïr déns

23 Mán goeth fórth to his wórk, and to his *lá*-bour : un-*tíl* the ëve-ning.

24 O Lórd, how mánifold are *thy* wórks : in wísdom hast thou máde them áll ; the eárth is fúll *of* thy rīch-es.

25 Só is the gréat and wíde sea *ál*-so : whérein are thíngs créeping innúmerable, both *small* and grëat béasts.

26 Thére go the shíps, and thére is that Leví-*a*-than : whom thóu hast máde to táke his *pás*-time thëre-in.

27 Thése wait áll up-*on* thée : that thou mayest gíve them méat *in* dúe sëa-son.

28 Whén thou gívest it thém they gá-*ther* it : and whén thou ópenest thy hánd they are *fíll*-ed wīth góod.

29 Whén thou hídest thy fáce they are *tróu*-bled : when thou tákest awáy their bréath they díe ; and are túrned a-*gáin* to theĭr dúst.

30 When thou léttest thy bréath go fórth they sháll *be* máde : and thóu shalt reńew the *fáce* of thë earth.

31 The glórious Majesty of the Lórd shall endúre for *év*-er : the Lórd shall re-*jóice* in hĭs wórks.

32 The˙eárth shall trémble at the loók *of* hím : if he dó but tóuch *the* hílls, thëy shall˄smóke.

33 I will síng unto the Lórd as lońg as *I* lĭve : I will praíse my Gód while I *háve* my bë-ing.

34 And só shall my wórds *pléase* him : my jóy shall *be* ín thë Lord.

35 As for sínners, they shall be consúmed óut of the éarth ; and the ungódly shall cóme to *an* énd : praíse thou the Lórd, Ó *my* śoul, praīse the^Lórd.

Glóry be to the Fáther, and to *the* Són : **and** *to* the Hö-ly^Ghóst.

As it wás in the begínning, is nów, and éver *sháll* be : wórld with-*óut* énd.   A-men.

PSALM 145   *Exaltabo te Deus*   TONE III

I WILL mágnify *thée*, O^Gód, my Kíng : and I will praíse thy Náme for *év*-er and év-er.

2 'Every dáy will I give *thánks* un-to thée : and praíse thy Náme for *év*-er and év-er.

3 Gréat is the Lórd, and márvellous-wórthy *to* be práis-ed : thére is no *énd* of his gréat-ness.

4 'One generátion shall praíse thy wórks un-*to* an-ó-ther : and *de*-cláre thy pów-er.

5 'As for mé, I will be tálking *of* thy wór-ship : thy glóry, *thy* práise, and wón-drous^wórks ;

6 So that mén shall spéak of the míght of thy *már*-vel-lous aćts : and I will álso *téll* of thy gréat-ness.

7 The memórial of thine abúndant kíndness *shall* be shéw-ed : and mén shall *sing* of thy rígh-teous⁼ness.

8 The Lórd is *grá*-cious,⌒and⌒mér-ci-ful : lóng-súffering, *and* of gréat góod-ness.

9 The Lórd is lóving *un*-to⌒év-ery mán : and his mércy *is* ó-ver áll his⌒wórks.

10 'All thy wórks *praise* thee, O Lórd : and thy saínts *give* thánks un-to thée.

11 They shéw the glóry *of* thy kíng-dom : and *tálk* of thy pów-er ;

12 That thy pówer, thy glóry, and míghtiness *of* thy kíng-dom : míght *be* knówn un-to mén.

13 Thy kíngdom is an ever-*lást*-ing kíng-dom : and thy domínion endúreth *through*-óut all áges.

14 The Lórd uphóldeth *all* súch as fáll : **and** lífteth up *all* thóse that are dówn.

15 The éyes of áll wáit up-*on* thée, O Lórd : and thou gívest them their *méat* in due séa-son.

16 Thou ó-pen⁼est thine hańd : and fíllest áll things *liv*-ing with plén-teous⁼ness.

17 The Lórd is *righ*-teous⌒in⌒áll his wáys : and *hó*-ly in áll his⌒wórks.

18 The Lórd is nígh unto áll thém that *cáll* up-ón him : yéa, all súch as cáll *up*-ón him fáith-ful⁼ly.

19 He will fulfíl the desíre of *thém* that féar him : he álso will héar their *crý*, and will hélp thém.

20 The Lórd presérveth all *thém* that lóve him : but scáttereth abróad *all* the un-gód-ly.

21 My móuth shall spéak the *praise* of the Lórd :

and let áll flésh give thánks unto his hóly Náme for *év*-er and év-er.

Glóry be to the *Fá*-ther,^and^to the Són : *and* to the Hó-ly^Ghóst.

As it wás in the begínning, is nów, and *év*-er sháll be : wórld *with*-óut énd.   A-men.

TONE I (*ornate form*)

MY SOÜL doth *mág*-ni-fy⌢the Lórd : and my spírit hath rejoíced in *Gód* my Sá-viour.

2 FOR HË *háth* re-gárd-ed : the lówliness of *his* hand-maíd-en.

3 FOR BË-*hóld* from hénce-forth : áll generá-tions shall *cáll* me bléss-ed.

4 FOR HË that is míghty hath *mág*-ni-fi⌐ed mé : and hó-*ly* is his Náme.

5 AND HÏS mércy is on *thém* that féar him : throughóut all *gé*-ne-rá-tions.

6 HE HÄTH shéwed *stréngth* with his árm : he hath scáttered the próud in the imaginá-*tion* of theír heárts.

7 HE HÄTH put dówn the *mígh*-ty⌢from their séat : and hath exálted the *húm*-ble and méek.

8 HE HÄTH fílled the *hún*-gry⌢with góod thíngs : and the rích he hath sent *émp*-ty a-wáy.

9 HE, RË-mémbering his mércy, hath hólpen his *sér*-vant 'Is⌐ra-el : as he prómised to óur fore-fáthers ; 'Abraham and his *séed* for év-er.

GLÓ-RŸ be to the *Fá*-ther⌢and to⌢the Són : and *to* the Hó-ly Ghóst.

AS ÏT wás in the begínning, is nów, and *év*-er sháll be : wórld with-*óut* énd.   A-men.

Tone II

Ending 1

Ending 2

MY SÓUL doth mágnify the *Lórd* : and my
spírit hath rejoíced in *Gód* my Sá-viour.

2 FOR HE háth re-*gárd*-ed : the lówliness of
his hand-maíd-en.

3 FOR BE-hóld, from *hénce*-forth : áll generá-
tions shall *cáll* me bléss-ed.

4 FOR HÉ that is míghty hath mágnified *mé* :
and hó-*ly* is his Náme.

5 AND HIS mércy is on thém that *féar* him :
throughóut all *gé*-ne-rá-tions.

6 HE HATH shéwed stréngth with his *árm* :
he hath scáttered the próud in the imáginá-*tion*
of theír héarts.

7 HE HATH put dówn the míghty from their
séat : and hath exálted the *húm*-ble and méek.

8 HE HATH fílled the húngry with góod
things : and the rích he hath sent *émp*-ty a-wáy.

9 HE, RE-mémbering his mércy, hath hólpen
his sérvant *'Is*-ra⁼el : as he prómised to óur fore-
fáthers ; 'Abraham and his *séed* for év-er.

GLÓ-RY be to the Fáther, and to the *Són* :
and *to* the Hó-ly Ghóst.

AS IT wás in the begínning, is nów, and éver
sháll be : wórld with-*óut* énd.   A-men.

Tone III

MY SÓUL doth *mág*-ni-fy the Lórd : and my spírit hath rejoíced in Gód *my* Sá-viour.

2 For he *háth* re-gárd-ed : the lówliness of his *hand*-maíd-en.

3 For be-*hóld* from hénce-forth : áll generátions shall cáll *me* bléss-ed.

4 FOR HÉ that is míghty hath *mág*-ni-fi-ed mé : and hóly *is* his Náme.

5 AND HIS mércy is on *thém* that féar him : throughóut all gé-*ne*-rá-tions.

6 HE HATH shéwed *stréngth* with his árm : he hath scáttered the próud in the imáginátion *of* theír heárts.

7 HE HATH put dówn the *migh*-ty^from their séat : and hath exálted the húm-*ble* and méek.

8 HE HATH fílled the *hún*-gry^with góod thíngs : and the rích he hath sent émp-*ty* a-wáy.

9 HE, RE-mémbering his mércy, hath hólpen his *sér*-vant 'Is-ra-el : as he prómised to óur fórefathers ; 'Abraham and his séed *for* év-er.

GLÓ-RY be to the *Fá*-ther,^and to the Són : and *to* the Hó-ly Ghóst.

AS IT wás in the begínning, is nów, and *év*-er sháll be : wórld withóut *énd*. A-men.

Tone IV

Ending 4

Ending 7

M Y SÓUL doth mágni-*fy* the Lórd : and my spírit hath rejoíced *in* Gód my Sá-viour.

2 For he *háth* re-gárd-ed : the lówliness *of* his hand-maíd-en.

3 For be-*hóld* from hénce-forth : áll generátions *shall* cáll me bléss-ed.

4 FOR HÉ that is míghty hath mágni-*fi*-ed mé : and *hó*-ly is his Náme.

5 AND HIS mércy is on *thém* that féar him : throughóut *all* gé-ne-rá-tions.

6 HE HATH shéwed stréngth *with* his árm : he hath scáttered the próud in the imági-*ná*-tion of theír héarts.

7 HE HATH put dówn the míghty *from* their séat : and hath exálted *the* húm-ble and méek.

8 HE HATH fílled the húngry *with* góod thíngs : and the rích he hath *sent* émp-ty a-wáy.

9 HE, RE-mémbering his mércy, hath hólpen his *sér*-vant 'Is-ra-el : as he prómised to óur forefáthers ; 'Abraham and *his* séed for év-er.

GLÓ-RY be to the Fáther, and *to* the Són : *and* to the Hó-ly Ghóst.

AS IT wás in the begínning, is nów, and *év*-er sháll be : wórld *with*-óut énd.　A-men.

TONE V

M Y SÓUL doth mágnify the *Lórd* : and my
spírit hath rejoíced in *Gód* my Sá-viour.

2 FOR HE háth re-*gárd*-ed : the lówliness of
his hand-maíd-en.

3 FOR BE-hóld, from *hénce*-forth : áll generá-
tions shall *cáll* me bléss-ed.

4 FOR HÉ that is míghty hath mágnified *mé* :
and hó-*ly* is his Náme.

5 AND HIS mércy is on thém that *féar* him :
throughóut all *gé*-ne-rá-tions.

6 HE HATH shéwed stréngth with his *árm* :
he hath scáttered the próud in the imáginá-*tion*
of theír héarts.

7 HE HATH put dówn the míghty from their
séat : and hath exálted the *húm*-ble and méek.

8 HE HATH fílled the húngry with góod
things : and the rích he hath sent *émp*-ty a-wáy.

9 HE, RE-mémbering his mércy, hath hólpen
his sérvant 'Is-ra-el : as he prómised to óur fore-
fáthers ; 'Abraham and his *séed* for év-er.

GLÓ-RY be to the Fáther, and to the *Són* :
and *to* the Hó-ly Ghóst.

AS IT wás in the begínning, is nów, and éver
sháll be : wórld with-*óut* énd.   A-men.

TONE VI (*ornate form*)

MY SOÜL doth *mág*-ni-fy⌢the Lórd : and my spírit hath rejoíced in *Gód* my Sá-viour.

2 FOR HË *háth* re-gárd-ed : the lówliness of *his* hand-maíd-en.

3 FOR BË-*hóld* from hénce-forth : áll generá-tions shall *cáll* me bléss-ed.

4 FOR HË that is míghty hath *mág*-ni-fi⌐ed mé : and hó-*ly* is his Náme.

5 AND HÏS mércy is on *thém* that féar him : throughóut all *gé*-ne-rá-tions.

6 HE HÄTH shéwed *stréngth* with his árm : he hath scáttered the próud in the imáginá-*tion* of theír heárts.

7 HE HÄTH put dówn the *migh*-ty⌢from their séat : and hath exálted the *húm*-ble and méek.

8 HE HÄTH fílled the *hún*-gry⌢with góod thíngs : and the rích he hath sent *émp*-ty a-wáy.

9 HE, RË-mémbering his mércy, hath hólpen his *sér*-vant 'Is⌐ra-el : as he prómised to óur fore-fáthers ; 'Abraham and his *séed* for év-er.

GLÓ-RŸ be to the *Fá*-ther⌢and to⌢the Són : and *to* the Hó-ly Ghóst.

AS ÏT wás in the begínning, is nów, and *év*-er sháll be : wórld with-*óut* énd.   A-men.

Tone VII

Ending 1

Ending 7

M Y SÓUL doth *mág*-ni-fy the Lórd : and my spírit hath rejoíced in *Gód* my Sá-viour.

2 For he *háth* re-gárd-ed : the lówliness of *his* hand-maíd-en.

3 For be-*hóld* from hénce-forth : áll generátions shall *cáll* me bléss-ed.

4 FOR HÉ that is míghty hath *mág*-ni-fi-ed mé : and *hó*-ly is his Náme.

5 AND HIS mércy is on *thém* that féar him : throughóut all *gé*-ne-rá-tions.

6 HE HATH shéwed *stréngth* with his árm : he hath scáttered the próud in the imági-*ná*-tion of theír heárts.

7 HE HATH put dówn the *mígh*-ty͡from their séat : and hath exálted the *húm*-ble and méek.

8 HE HATH fílled the *hún*-gry͡with góod thíngs : and the rích he hath sent *émp*-ty a-wáy.

9 HE, RE-mémbering his mércy, hath hólpen his *sér*-vant 'Is-ra-el : as he prómised to óur fórefathers ; 'Abraham and his *séed* for év-er.

GLÓ-RY be to the *Fá*-ther,͡and to the Són : and *to* the Hó-ly Ghóst.

AS IT wás in the beginning, is nów, and *év*-er sháll be : wórld with-*out* énd. **A-men.**

Tone VIII

M Y SÓUL doth mágnify the *Lórd* : and my
spírit hath rejoíced in *Gód* my Sá-viour.

2 FOR HE háth re-*gárd*-ed : the lówliness of
his hand-maíd-en.

3 FOR BE-hóld, from *hénce*-forth : áll generá-
tions shall *cáll* me bléss-ed.

4 FOR HÉ that is míghty hath mágnified *mé* :
and hó-*ly* is his Náme.

5 AND HIS mércy is on thém that *féar* him :
throughóut all *gé*-ne-rá-tions.

6 HE HATH shéwed stréngth with his *árm* :
he hath scáttered the próud in the imáginá-*tion*
of theír héarts.·

7 HE HATH put dówn the míghty from their
séat : and hath exálted the *húm*-ble and méek.

8 HE HATH fílled the húngry with góod
things : and the rích he hath sent *émp*-ty a-wáy.

9 HE, RE-mémbering his mércy, hath hólpen
his sérvant *'Is*-ra-el : as he prómised to óur fore-
fáthers ; *'Abraham* and his *séed* for év-er.

GLÓ-RY be to the Fáther, and to the *Són* :
and *to* the Hó-ly Ghóst.

AS IT wás in the begínning, is nów, and éver
sháll be : wórld with-*óut* énd. · A-men.

Tone I

LÓRD, NOW léttest thou thy sérvant
depárt *in* péace : accórd-*ing* to thý wórd.

2 FOR MINE éyes *have* séen : thy sal-vá-tion.

3 WHICH THÓU hást pre-*pár*-ed : befóre the
fáce *of* all peó-ple.

4 TO BE a líght to líghten the *Gén*-tiles : and
to be the glóry of thy *péo*-ple 'Is-ra-el.

GLÓ-RY be to the Fáther, and to *the* Són :
and *to* the Hó-ly Ghóst.

AS IT wás in the begínning, is nów, and éver
sháll be : wórld with-*óut* énd.   A-men.

Tone II

LÓRD, NOW léttest thou thy sérvant depárt
in *péace* : accórding *to* thý wórd.

2 FOR MINE éyes have *séen* : thy *sal*-vá-tion.

3 WHICH THÓU hást pre-*pár*-ed : befóre the
fáce of *all* peó-ple.

4 TO BE a líght to líghten the *Gén*-tiles : and
to be the glóry of thy péo-*ple* 'Is-ra-el.

GLÓ-RY be to the Fáther, and to the *Són* :
and to *the* Hó-ly Ghóst.

AS IT wás in the begínning, is nów, and éver
sháll be : wórld withóut *énd*.   A-men.

L

Tone III

LÓRD, NOW léttest thóu thy *sér*-vant⌒
de⌐párt in péace : ac-*córd*-ing to thý wórd.
2 *For* mine éyes have séen :—— thy sal-vá-tion.
3 Which thou *hást* pre-pár-ed : befóre the *fáce*
of all péo-ple.
4 TÓ BÉ a líght to *líght*-en⌒the Gén-tiles : and
to be the glóry of *thy* péo-ple 'Is-ra⌐el.
GLÓ-RY be to the *Fá*-ther,⌒and⌒to the Són :
and to the Hó-ly⌒Ghóst.
AS IT wás in the begínning, is nów, and *év*-er
sháll be : wórld *with*-óut énd.   A-men.

Tone IV

LÓRD, NOW léttest thou thy sérvant de-
párt in péace : accórding to *thÿ* wórd.
2 For mine *éyes* have séen : thy sal-*vä*-tion.
3 Which thou *hást* pre-pár-ed : befóre the fáce
of all *péó*-ple.
4 TÓ BÉ a líght to líght-*en* the Gén-tiles : and
to be the glóry of thy péople *Iȝ*-ra⌐el.
GLÓ-RY be to the Fáther, and *to* the Són :
and to the *Hö*-ly⌒Ghóst.
AS IT wás in the begínning, is nów, and *év*-er
sháll be : wórld withóut énd.   *Á*-men.

TONE V

LORD, NOW léttest thou thy sérvant depárt in *péace* : ac-*córd*-ing to thý wórd.

2 FOR MINE éyes have *séen* : thy sal-vá-tion.

3 WHICH THOU hást pre-*pár*-ed : befóre the *fáce* of all péo-ple.

4 TO BE a líght to líghten the *Gén*-tiles : and to be the glóry of thy *péo*-ple 'Is-ra-el.

GLO-RY be to the Fáther, and to the *Són* : and *to* the Hó-ly Ghóst.

AS IT wás in the begínning, is nów, and éver *sháll* be : wórld with-*óut* énd.   A-men.

TONE VI

LÓRD, NOW léttest thóu thy *sér*-vant˄ de-párt˄in péace : accórd-*ing* tö thý wórd.

2 *For* mine éyes˄have séen : *thy* säl-vá-tion.

3 Which thou *hást* pre-pár-ed : befóre the fáce *of* äll péo-ple.

4 TO BE a líght to *líght*-en˄the Gén-tiles : and to be the glóry of thy *péo*-plë 'Is-ra˄el.

GLO-RY be to the *Fá*-ther,˄and to˄the Són : and *to* thë Hó-ly˄Ghóst.

AS IT wás in the begínning, is nów, and *év*-er sháll be : wórld with-*óut* ënd.   A-men.

Tone VII

LORD, now léttest thou thy *sér*-vant⁀de-
párt⁀in péace : ac-*córd*-ing to thý wórd.

2 *For* mine éyes⁀have séen : *thy* sal-vá-tion.

3 Which thou *hást* pre-pár-ed : befóre the fáce
of all péo-ple.

4 TO BE a líght to *light*-én⁀the Gén-tiles : and
to be the glóry of thy *péo*-ple 'Is-ra-el.

GLÓ-RY be to the *Fá*-ther,⁀and to⁀the Són :
and *to* the Hó-ly Ghóst.

AS IT wás in the begínning, is nów, and *év*-er
sháll be : wórld with-*óut* énd.   A-men.

Tone VIII

LÓRD, NOW léttest thou thy sérvant depárt
in *péace* : accórd-*ing* to thý wórd.

2 FOR MINE éyes have *séen* : *thy* sal-vá-tion.

3 WHICH THOU hást pre-*pár*-ed : befóre
the fáce *of* all péo-ple.

4 TO BE a líght to líghten the *Gén*-tiles : and
to be the glóry of thy *péo*-ple 'Is-ra-el.

GLÓ-RY be to the Fáther, and to the *Són* :
and *to* the Hó-ly⁀Ghóst.

AS IT wás in the begínning, is nów, and éver
sháll be : wórld with-*óut* énd.   A-men.

OUR Father, which art in heaven, Hallowed be thy name; Thy kingdom come; Thy will be done; In earth as it is in Heaven. Give us this day our daily bread. And forgive us our trespasses, As we forgive them that trespass against us. And lead us not into temptation; But deliver us from evil: For thine is the kingdom, the power, and the glory, For ever and ever. Amen.

PRIEST. **ANSWER.**

O Lórd, o - pen thóu our lips.   And our móuth shall shew fórth

PRIEST. **ANSWER.**

thy praise.   O Gód, make spéed to sáve us.   O Lórd, make

PRIEST.

háste to hélp us.   Gló - ry be to the ·Fá-ther, and tó the Són :

ANSWER.

and tó the Hó - ly Ghóst.   As it wás in the be - gín-ning, is nów, and

PRIEST.

év - er sháll be : wórld with-out énd.   A-mén. Praise ye the Lórd.

ANSWER.

The Lórd's Náme be praí - sed.

*   *   *   *   *   *   *   *   *

I BELIEVE in God the Father Almighty, Maker of heaven and earth:
And in Jesus Christ his only Son our Lord, Who was conceived
by the Holy Ghost, Born of the Virgin Mary, Suffered under Pontius
Pilate, Was crucified, dead, and buried, He descended into hell;
The third day he rose again from the dead, He ascended into heaven,
And sitteth on the right hand of God the Father Almighty; From
thence he shall come to judge the quick and the dead. I believe in
the Holy Ghost; The Holy Catholick Church; The Communion of
Saints; The Forgiveness of sins;

PRIEST.　　　　　　　　　　　　ANSWER.

The ré - sur - réc-tion of the bó - dy, and the life ev - er-last-ing. A-men.

PRIEST.　　　　　　ANSWER.　　　　　　PRIEST.

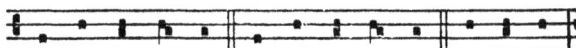

The Lórd be with you. And with thy spí - rit. Let us pray.

ANSWER.

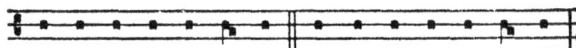

Lórd, have mér - cy up - ón us. Christ, have mér - cy up - ón us.

Lórd, have mér-cy up - ón us.

O UR Father, which art in heaven, Hallowed be thy name; Thy
kingdom come; Thy will be done; In earth as it is in heaven.
Give us this day our daily bread. And forgive us our trespasses,
As we forgive them that trespass against us,

PRIEST.　　　　　　　　　　　ANSWER.

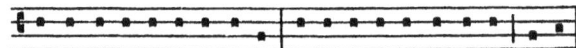

and léad us nót in - to temptá-tion, Bút de - lív- er us from é - vil. A - men.

PRIEST.   ANSWER.

O Lórd, shew thy mér - cy up - ón us.   And gránt us thy sal - vá - tion.

PRIEST.   ANSWER.

O Lórd, sáve the Queen   And mér - ci - ful - ly héar us when we cáll up - on thée.

PRIEST.   ANSWER.

En - dúe thy mín - is - ters with rígh-teous-ness.   And máke thy chó - sen

PRIEST.   ANSWER.

péo-ple jóy-ful.   O Lórd, sáve thy péo-ple.   And bléss thine in - hé - ri-tance.

PRIEST.   ANSWER.

Give peáce in our tíme, O Lórd.   Be-cáuse there is none ó - ther that

PRIEST.

fight-eth for ús, but ón - ly thóu, O Gód.   O Gód, make cléan our

ANSWER.   *After the Collects.*

heárts with-ín us.   And táke not thy hó - ly Spí - rit fróm us.   A-men.

CELEBRANT   ANSWER

The Lórd be with you.   And with thy spí - rit.

CANTORS   ANSWER

℣. Let us bléss the Lórd. ℟. Thánks be to Gód.

TE DEUM LAUDAMUS

Modes iij & iv

We práise thee, O God: we ac-knów-ledge thee to be the Lórd.

PIETRO ALFIERI.

All the éarth doth wór - ship thee: the Fá - ther

ev - er - - lást - - - - - ing.

To thée all Án-gels crý a-lóud: the Heavens, and áll the Pówers therein.

To thée Ché-ru-bim and Sé-

-ra-phim: con-tín-ual-ly do cry.

Hó-ly:

Ho — — — — — — — ly,

Hó — — — — — — — ly,

Hó-ly, Lórd Gód of Sa-bá-oth.

Héa-ven and éarth are fúll of the má-jes-ty of thy gló - rý.

The gló - ri - ous cóm-pa - ny of the A - pó-stles práise thee.

The góod - ly fél - low - ship of the

Pró - phets práise . . . . . . thee.

The nó - ble ár - my of Már - tyrs práise thee.

The Hó - ly Chúrch through - out áll the wórld

doth ac - knów - - - . ledge thee.

The Fá - ther of an ín - fi - nite Má - jes - ty.

Thine hó - nour - a - ble, trúe and ón - ly Són.

Al - so the Hó - ly Ghóst the Cóm - fort - er.

Thóu art the Kíng of gló - ry, O . . . Chríst.

Thóu art the év - er - lást - ing Són of the Fá - ther.

Whén thou tóokest up - ón thee to de - lí - ver man:

thóu didst . . nót ab - hór the Vír - gin's wómb.

When thóu hadst o - ver - cóme the shárp - ness of déath:

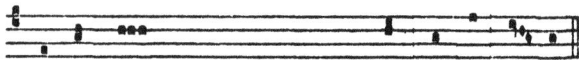

thou didst ó - pen the kíng-dom of héav'n to áll be - líev - ers.

Thou síttestat the right hánd of Gód: in the

gló - ry of the Fá - - - ther.

We be - líeve that thóu shalt cóme to bé our Júdge.

We thérefore práy thee, hélp thy sér - vants: whom thou hást redéemed with thy

pré - - - - - - - cious Blóod.

Máke them to be núm-ber'd with thy Sáints in gló - ry ev - er - lást - ing.

O Lórd, sáve thy péo - - ple and bléss thine hé - ri - tage.

182

Góv - ern them, and líft them úp for év - er.

Dáy by dáy we mág - ni - fy thee.

And we wór - ship thy Náme, ev - er wórld with - out énd.

Vouch - sáfe, O Lórd, to kéep us this dáy with - out .. sín. . .

O Lórd, have mér - cy up - ón us: have mér - cy up - ón us.

O Lórd, let thy mércy líghten up - ón us: as our trúst is in .. thee.

O Lórd, in thée have I trúst - ed:

let me név - er be con - fóund - ed.

℣. Let us bléss the Fáther, and the Són, with the Hóly Spí - rit

℟. Let us práise him and mágnify him for - - - - - év - er

℣. Bléssed art thóu, O Lórd, in the fírmament - - - - - of héaven,

℟. And híghly to be práised, and glórious, and mágnified for év - er

℣. O Lórd, - - - - - - - - - - - - - héar my práyer.

℟. And lét my crýing come - - - - - - - - - - ún - to thée.

℣. The Lórd be with you.

℟. And with thý spírit.

Let us pray.

COLLECT.

O GOD, whose mercies cannot be numbered, whose goodness passeth man's understanding ; we render humble and hearty thanks to thy most gracious majesty for the gifts that thou hast bestowed upon us : humbly beseeching thy mercy, that like as thou hast at this time heard the prayers of them that call upon thee, so thou wouldest hereafter evermore dispose the way of thy servants towards the attainment of everlasting life. Through Jesus Christ our Lord. ℟. Amen.

Mode I

Gód be in my héad, and in my un - der - stánd - ing;

Gód be in my éyes, and in my lóok - ing;

Gód be in my móuth, and in my spéak - ing;

Gód be in my héart, and in my thínk - ing;

Gód be at my ' énd, and at my de - párt - ing.

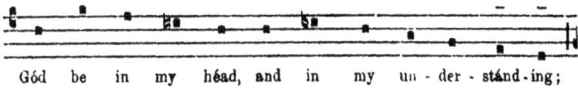

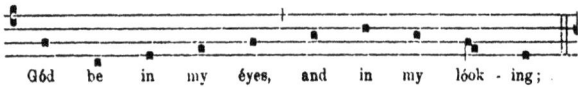

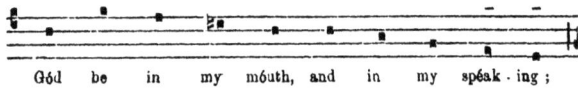

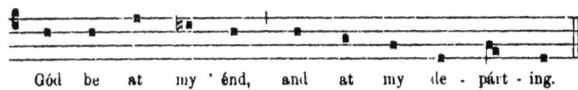

Words from the SARUM
PRIMER of 1558

www.ingramcontent.com/pod-product-compliance
Lightning Source LLC
Chambersburg PA
CBHW052001090426
42741CB00008B/1489